MY LIFE AS A REAR END

|◄+++++++++►|

MY LIFE
AS A
REAR END

Memoirs of a
Train Conductor

┣━┿━┿━┿━┿━┿━┿━┿━┫

PAUL HOLLAND

TABLE OF CONTENTS

|◄-◄-◄-◄-◄-◄-►-►-►|

Preface

TRAIN OF THOUGHT

B OY HAVE I GOT A STORY TO TELL YOU! THE
crazy part is that all the railroad stories in this book
are true. Any slight deviations from reality are so as to
ensure anonymity. Opinions if any, are my own and do
not express the viewpoints of any individual railroad or
rail employees. Despite the admitted craziness of my experiences, the riding public should have no apprehension
about riding our railroads. The vast majority of my experiences preceded the advent and implementation of major

safety and security improvements, including but certainly not limited to event recorders (black boxes), audio and video surveillance and much to my personal chagrin, nationwide drug and alcohol testing.

This story will in all likelihood start and end with the same emotion, that being affection. There were definite exceptions which will follow, but for the most part it was thirty-eight years of love for the railroad. Love for my co-workers, love for my commuters and most of all love for my wife and kids who wouldn't be here if I hadn't met my wife on the train. I often tell her that other than one really special umbrella, she's the best thing I ever found on a train. Hey it wasn't just any umbrella. Hit the button and it opened. Hit the button again and it automatically closed. It had me mesmerized, just like my wife. She's actually a lot better than an automatic umbrella but I don't want her getting a big head.

Unlike many train conductors and locomotive engineers, I had no family on the railroad. And unlike some railroaders, I will be a one hit wonder in that my children will probably not follow me onto the rails. While other dads were with their families, my kids knew I would be working every Christmas, Thanksgiving, New Year's and more. Most kids arise early Christmas morning because they are excited to open their presents. My kids got up at 4:00 a.m. on Christmas because it was our only opportunity to be together on Christmas morning. They saw the pressure of not being allowed to call in sick or be able to arrive late for work since work would literally leave without me. I'll always feel guilty about my hours preventing me from participating like other fathers did in Boy and Girl Scout meetings or coaching my kid's teams. I consider myself unbelievably lucky to have been a train conductor and I'm definitely not complaining. Just trying to paint a picture explaining why after seeing their dad work six and very often seven days a week for over three decades, the kids decided college afforded the potential for a better lifestyle. Speaking of luck, despite missing more family events than I could ever count, I was incredibly fortunate to have been present for the birth of all three of my kids. Luckily, all three times my wife went into labor I wasn't working on board a train. The train can't operate without an engineer and conductor and they aren't pulling over because of a family emergency.

Friends have asked how being a railroad conductor could be so funny. The truth is that life is funny. Just ask a funeral director. I learned to laugh thanks to my family and comedians like Mel Brooks who would have fit right in as one of my uncles. As far as I can recall it all started with my grandmothers. One grandma was named Grapes. Sadie Grapes. My other grandma was named Weiner. Minnie Weiner. You read that right. Mini Weiner. Grandma's Weiner and Grapes. Go figure. My parents were hard workers and made do during difficult financial times. My Dad, after his discharge from the War where he received the Bronze Star in the Battle of the Bulge in Germany, became a proud union clothes cutter in New York's Garment Center. Unfortunately, he cut maternity clothes. Picture an eight year old boy saving the family a few bucks by wearing maternity shorts and you know why I got beat up so much in school. Shortly after my birth, Hillside Hospital where I was born was converted into a mental hospital. Certainly explains a lot.

MY LIFE AS A REAR END

⊢⊣⊢⊣⊢⊣⊢⊣⊢⊣

WHO'S DRIVING THIS THING?

 ┣━━━━━━━┫

PERCHANCE YOU ACQUIRED THIS BOOK BECAUSE the cover caught your eye. If so, I know what you're thinking. Do these uniform pants make my ass look fat? Sorry, that's what I'm thinking. You are likely wondering if the conductor is on the rear end, who's driving the train? Regardless of where they board, be it an affluent town or a station with an insane asylum, passengers never seem to grasp the fact that conductors don't drive trains. The short answer to that inane question is that the engineer is operating the train, not the conductor. There's no shortage of dumb questions posed to train conductors. Every conductor has had a train parked right up against a wall or bumping block only to be asked, "Which way does this train go"? How can you not sarcastically respond that the building lifts up and the train goes right under the building? Or how about the passengers who complain that the front car is always too crowded? I explain that folks want to be the first one off the train and closest to the exit so there's nothing we can do about it. They invariably respond that we should add more cars to the front to alleviate the problem. I'll give you a minute to think about that one. The front car will always be the front car regardless of how many cars are on the train and therefore will always be packed. My favorite question of all time was when a woman approached me with panic written all over her face as she asked, "Which train bathroom has the most toilet paper"? Did she really think that her conductor counted the squares of toilet paper in each john prior to departure? More importantly, why did she want to know? Another beauty is when I'm standing next to my train in full regalia, complete with uniform jacket, ticket punch, money pouch, and hat that incidentally says "conductor" on it and a passenger walks up to me and asks "Are you a conductor"? No, I'm an ice cream man. What would you like? Chocolate Éclair or Rocky Road? Of course I'm a conductor!

And now the piece de resistance and question number one. "If you're here taking my ticket, who's driving the train"? I'm no Einstein but I've known the difference between a train conductor and locomotive engineer since I was a little kid. I continue to be amazed at how many people think the conductor drives the train. The duties of both conductor and engineer are much more complex than riders realize. The training for both crafts is extensive and quite daunting. The amount of information that has to be learned and retained is extensive and many folks fail to make it through training. I wish I had a dime for every time I received a sarcastic comment from a commuter because the train missed its regular spot on a platform by a few inches. In truth, with metal wheels and metal tracks it's a wonder we stop at all. I try not to think about the tiny wheel flange that is incredibly all that keeps a train from derailing. A mile long freight train, which is not unusual, traveling 55 miles per hour would take approximately 18 football fields to come to a stop. The operation of a freight train requires significant skills. Braking without derailing and accelerating without splitting the cars apart is not as easy as it looks. Passenger trains are no day at the beach either. Especially when commuters have no idea how difficult it is to bring a train to a smooth stop without spilling their coffee or knocking down standees. Passengers are always amazed during leaf season when braking and accelerating can become virtually impossible during a light mist. A chemical in the leaves bonds with a chemical in the steel rail so as to form a compound that is unbelievably slippery. Even our best engineers are at times left helpless during "slip, slide season". Passenger and freight train engineers must remain fixated on safely operating their train regardless of the season. The potential for catastrophic destruction caused by freight train accidents is well documented and passenger train engineers have the lives of hundreds of passengers in their hands at all times. They must remain focused on speed limits based on their territory (there are usually no speed limit signs), signals, curves, track restrictions, work zones, equipment restrictions and much, much more. Every individual train, even of the same type, reacts differently to their command to brake or accelerate. The slightest slip up by an engineer could result in the loss of his or her job or tragically, the loss of life. A conductor on the other hand, never drives a train but does control its movement when the engineer is operating from somewhere other than the head end of their train. This occurs during reverse movements or when the controls in the lead car or engine become defective in route. In that case, the conductor becomes the eyes and ears of the engineer and keeps the emergency brake valve (referred to as the dump valve) nearby at all times. The dump valve is the only means by which the conductor may bring the train to a stop. The conductor, like the engineer, must be well versed on all the characteristics of the territory on which he or she works. In addition to having knowledge of the territory, the freight conductor is in charge of the carloads, switches, handbrakes, operation of locomotives through the use of remote control devices, compliance with all Federal Railroad Administration and their railroad's rules, regulations and more. A passenger conductor is not only familiar with the territory but also ensures the safety and comfort of the passengers. They are responsible for the actions and safety of the crew and for reporting any unsafe conditions. Making announcements, operating the doors, setting up the coaches, ensuring fares are collected, coupling and uncoupling cars, throwing rail switches, troubleshooting equipment breakdowns, providing flag protection for workers on the tracks and providing for safe train evacuations in emergencies are just a few of their duties. Due to the need for the engineer to have all of his or her attention focused on the operation of the train, they cannot be responsible for the actions of the rest of the crew nor the needs of the passengers. That's one of the reasons the conductor is in charge of the entire crew. Conductors like myself could have become engineers and engineers could transfer to conductor if they thought it preferable. Truth be told, not everyone is cut out for every job. Not every conductor has the necessary focus to be an engineer and not every engineer possesses the required people skills to handle customer service and supervise a crew. Conductors and engineers definitely form a bond and understandably get a few weird looks when referring to each other, regardless of gender, as each other's "train wife". No engineer or conductor looks forward to having their regular partner take a day off resulting in them having to work with a new railroader. For the most part the substitutes are excellent but there were certainly a few exceptions. On one memorable occasion I received a last minute replacement engineer. The new engineer had never operated alone on the territory and literally cried the entire trip. We arrived twenty minutes late and I had to come up with some creative excuses so as not to get the new engineer in trouble for delaying the train due to being scared half to death. Toward the end of my career, with thirty-seven years under my belt, I had a new engineer with just a few months on the job try to tell me that virtually everything I was doing was incorrect, and we hadn't even left the sign-in room yet! As we headed out to our train I couldn't help but notice that the new engineer was walking to the rear of the train instead of the head end. Mr. Know-it-all apparently thought he had all the answers but didn't know which end of the train to drive from. Needless to say, that turned into an eventful day. I wanted to punch my regular engineer in the nose for taking the day off. The truth is we rely on each other to stay out of trouble and more importantly we need each other to ensure our safety and the safety of the public. In short, the conductor conducts the train and the engineer operates it.

CRAZY FOR YOU

├─┼─┼─┼─┼─┼─┤

TAKE A TRAIN STATION AND PLACE IT DIRECTLY across the street from a hospital for the criminally insane. What could possibly go wrong? For over seven decades, one of New York State's largest mental hospitals was located at one of our train stations. In addition to housing a significantly demented segment of society, this hospital had the unfortunate distinction of being in the vanguard of frontal lobotomy surgery. Were it not for the tragic consequences of some people battling mental illness, this one train station had enough material for a great sitcom or reality show. I would like to think the relationships forged between our train crews and the patients made a genuine difference in their lives. I know for sure they impacted our conductors, often in a way that left them laughing. Comically, at times the line some-times blurred between conductors and cuckoos. One en-terprising young man managed to break out of one of the more secure buildings and boarded our train. Not having any funds for his train fare, he somehow convinced our conductor that he was a railroad employee who had for-gotten his pass. Apparently he used the same ruse to make his way onto an Amtrak train out of New York's Penn Station. The resourceful escapee made his way all the way to Boston, and was finally caught and returned to the hospital after trying to sneak into a Red Sox baseball game. Amazingly, he wasn't the only inpatient to not only find his way onto the wrong side of the fence but also into a short lived career on the railroad. Many years ago the story was told of a conductor who was relieved to finally have an assistant conductor aboard his train to offer his assistance collecting the fares. His relief was short-lived, as it didn't take long to realize his new helper was a few slices short of a loaf. Apparently this young fellow's fam-ily asked a retiring conductor if he would give their son who was a patient in the mental hospital his conductor's hat. Being a nice guy who obviously no longer had a use for it, the retiree gave the family not only his hat but also his entire uniform. Sure enough, the young fellow found a way through the fence and made his way to the station as our railroad's newest, phony conductor. The young lad was only able to collect enough money for cigarettes be-fore a passenger called him on his ruse. The real conduc-tor told him to beat it with the understanding that he change his clothes and return to surrender the uniform in which case no one would be made the wiser. Sure enough, there he was on the platform the next day, uniform in hand. The railroad would have been displeased to know the conductor was an old softy and let the young man keep the hat.

There were occasions when I admittedly failed to cut enough slack for the folks who were living on a different mental planet. One afternoon a woman boarded who at first seemed relatively stable but as I tried to collect her fare she became more and more belligerent. For some reason, she struck me the wrong way and we got into a rip-roaring argument. We looked like two dogs arguing in the aisle barking at each other. I completely lost it, as did she. My engineer that day was well over six feet tall and quite husky. He looked a lot like Santa Claus only larger. Apparently he, and everyone else in the train car heard me going at it with the passenger. He dumped the train, thereby applying the brakes, left his operating cab and came charging down the aisle. The engineer literally lifted me into the air and carried me up front to the cab while the passengers looked on in amazement. He put me back down and said, "Are you arguing with that lady? *Yes.* Did she get on at the last station? *Yes.* Did she come out of the nuthouse? *Yes.* Is she a loony tune? *Yes.* Why the hell are you arguing with someone who is crazy!?!?" That one dumb incident stayed with me the rest of my career and I tried to never let a nut-job bother me again. Thank you Santa.

My railroad claim to fame was the fact that I was the

only conductor in the history of our railroad to have his train hijacked. I'd like to thank the Academy (of dementia) for that award but I couldn't have done it without that crazy station. While it's true that this branch line included the mental asylum, it also included some of the most beautiful flora and fauna on our railroad. It traveled through an area that is so renowned that it was featured in National Geographic. I observed black bears, bobcats, otters, many kinds of turtles and every indigenous bird of prey, including the only snowy owl I've ever seen in the wild. For some reason long ago forgotten, I was going through a stressful period in my life and this territory was a great spot for lowering your blood pressure. When I reported for my first night on the assignment I was dismayed to see whom my engineer was. I liked him but he was known for his temper and for being extremely high strung. I explained to him that I only took that run to relax and he needed to stay calm. If we saw a turtle stuck on the tracks, he was to stop the train and I'd get out and help the little fella out. Just stay calm and have fun. He replied that he was on his meds, he enjoyed working with me and he would be fine. That lasted all of one trip.

The station where the mental hospital was located was on a single section of track governed by railroad rules known as Manual Block. Since trains operated in both directions on the same, single track, we were required to have written permission to occupy that section of railroad. Without that permission, a head on collision would have been likely. The cuckoo house was located at the

third station on the line but we were only authorized to stop at the first two stations and then reverse direction and head back. Since a train was heading directly towards us on the same track, that directive was not optional. As I walked through the train collecting tickets, a woman presented a ticket for the third stop. I punched it for a transfer and told her the second stop was our last and she would need to wait an hour for the next train. She insisted she was going to the third stop. I laughed and told her that she could insist all she wanted but the second stop would be our last. At that point she got up from her seat and pulled out a large switchblade knife. She held it to my throat and let me know in no uncertain terms that I was taking her to the third station. I was shaking like a leaf but I told her "You're right! We're going to your station". Meanwhile I knew there was no way we could do that without colliding head on with the southbound train. I slipped away from her and headed up to the engineer, who as I said earlier was not exactly known for being cool, calm and collected. As soon as I told him what had transpired he exploded like a lunatic. We were in enough trouble and I could have lived without that. We had no cell phones back then so I radioed to the dispatcher what had happened. He was a friend of mine but he didn't believe me and couldn't stop laughing. In the meantime, the woman kept waving the knife around which caused the passengers to crowd up front with us in an effort to get away from her. Someone working in a train yard heard the panic in my voice and called for the police. We arrived in the next town, which one might refer to as a shit-kicker village. The railroad police were unavailable and the one local officer who arrived at the scene looked like Andy Griffith's cousin. Fortunately, when he confronted the hijacker she was calmly sitting in her seat eating a bologna sandwich that she had apparently just cut in half with the switchblade. When the police report came out, it stated that her intent was to "break in" to the mental hospital. She got her wish, and I needed new underwear.

I am thankful to have retired never having experienced having a gun pulled on me. Unlike several co-workers, I was also fortunate to have never been spat on when involved in a passenger confrontation. A more positive event that I retired without experiencing was the on-board delivery of a baby. I did however deal with a plethora of medical emergencies while en route. The most memorable involved a poor fellow experiencing what appeared to be all the signs of a heart attack. The nearest assistance was several minutes away so I made a P.A. announcement requesting that any medical professionals on-board please make themselves known to the conductor. Sure enough, heading down the aisle from the front of the train came a tall dashing gentleman who identified himself as a cardiologist. As he began to check on the passenger a second individual arrived from the rear of the train. He brushed right by me without saying a word and shoved the first doctor out of the way. The initial doctor became irate and attempted to resume aiding the passenger but the second guy once again pushed him away while announcing that he was a neurosurgeon and he was taking over. My initial thought that this passenger may have been the luckiest guy in the world gave way to horror as the two doctors abandoned the rider and appeared ready to duke it out. However, as they argued, a third guy appeared. He looked like a character out of a Marx Brothers movie and looked nothing like a physician. He did however claim to be a doctor and calmed the passenger while the other two fellows argued behind him. I honestly believe that at best he was a veterinarian or more likely a complete nut but he stayed with the victim until the arrival of the paramedics. Here's a guy having a heart attack and instead of being treated by the neurosurgeon or cardiologist he was being treated by Groucho Marx. The lucky rider recovered, returned to work and lived to laugh about the incident and his good fortune.

THE WHEELS ON THE BUS
(& train) GO ROUND N' ROUND

O UR INSANE ASYLUM STATION WAS NOT THE
only stop where the vast majority of mental eleva-
tors never reached the top floor. One of our lines traveled
through a town that is tiny and extremely poor. In addition, the town folk keep to themselves and many of them
are related, resulting in a gene pool that's more like a hot
tub. An incident in that little village resulted in my only
trip inside the inner sanctum of the railroad superintendent's office. A young fellow's auto was struck at the
town's only grade crossing, resulting in the loss of his life.
Investigators were certain it was a suicide because the car
was parked on the tracks and the keys were removed from
the ignition. The superintendent had summoned me to

his office to tell me that the townsfolk refused to believe the results of the investigation and were threatening to shoot at our trains. I asked him how we were to protect ourselves and he said he had no idea but felt obligated to warn us. We weren't shot at but the next few trips gave new meaning to the word paranoia as I ducked down while making my way through the aisles.

While that little town certainly takes the cake for crazies, we actually had an entire branch line that kept life interesting. The area is an enigma in that despite it being one of the prettiest regions of the state, with some of the nicest people on our entire railroad, it also has a large element of crime, drug use and mental wackjobs. At times, the folks who rode those trains turned it into a virtual mental asylum on wheels. It didn't take long for me to realize I was in bizzaro world. On my first train, a young woman sat down directly across from me. She seemed articulate, attractive and intelligent. We chitchatted and since she appeared to be wearing hospital scrubs I asked what she did for a living. She replied that she was a nurse at a local hospital. As we made small talk, I happened to glance down and noticed that she wasn't wearing any shoes. All she had on her feet were woolen non-slip hospital socks. As our conversation progressed I realized she also had a hospital band on her wrist. I gave a wink wink, nudge nudge and said, "You aren't really a nurse, are you"? She sheepishly responded that she had just walked away from a psych ward. Welcome to the branch.

This branch line has historically and unfairly been

neglected, resulting in train service that was definitely sub-par. Due to frequent breakdowns and track work, the trains are often temporarily replaced with buses. At one point, the governor actually planned to pave over the train tracks and create a "busway". Fortunately, he was kicked out of office and imprisoned for other reasons prior to getting his plan approved. For ten straight weeks, due to a major bridge replacement project, I operated as a train conductor on the buses. I collected the train fares and helped the passengers with their train connections. Every single day on the buses was an adventure. The lack of female (and male) talent was immediately obvious. I'm very susceptible to motion sickness, so spending thirteen hours a day on a bus was about the stupidest move this train conductor could make. It was a run that was very lucrative so I took it anyway. On one of my first trips I was empathizing with a junkie that was throwing up in the front of the bus, much to the chagrin of the driver. Over his noise I heard what sounded like moaning coming from the rear of the bus. I walked back only to see the most gruesome woman you could ever imagine moaning and touching herself while reading what was at the time a brand new novel titled Fifty Shades of Gray. Retching in the front, coming in the back. Welcome to my world. She was probably the only one on the bus who knew how to read. One fellow each morning would board with his Daily News and end up passing the paper throughout the bus. I couldn't figure out how so many passengers could share just one newspaper so quickly until I realized that most of them were illiterate and only looking at the pictures. The paper would eventually make its way to me, so I really shouldn't complain. It took several weeks, but I finally saw what appeared to be the first hot woman heading toward my bus. She had a great figure and beautiful hair. It wasn't until she got closer that I realized she had a physical deformity that caused her lips to look like Daffy Duck's. I couldn't help thinking that she still might be a candidate in a beauty pageant up there. In fact the best pair of tits I saw on the buses belonged to a guy. I wish I were kidding. That's not to say all of the women were ugly. One 34-year-old woman was particularly attractive but I was a little taken aback when she told me that she was a grandmother by the time she turned 33.

Toward the end of the month, passengers on this branch line would run out of cash and try to barter for the fare. Can I just give you two sticks of gum?

Just get on the train!

I ran out of money because I needed to buy a new piece. I asked what he meant by a piece and he replied, "a gun, you idiot".

Just get on the train!

I'll blow you in the back of the train for the fare.

Just get on the train! (She had no teeth so a few devious thoughts crept into my head, but nah), *Just get on the train!*

One morning, my assistant got into a rip-roaring argument with a rider over a fare. I don't think she stood five feet tall and she was arguing with a guy who looked like a Neanderthal. He looked like he could snap both of our necks in a second. I got between them and made a time out motion with my hands. I asked her what the dispute was about and she said he had a monthly ticket that belonged to a female. The tickets are marked by gender because they are not transferable. I drew him away from her with a piece of beef jerky and asked him if there was a reason why he had a female ticket. This tough looking, scary as hell, 6'5" monster replied that he is a cross-dresser and usually boards as a woman.

Just get on the train!

We stopped at one station and a big guy boarded. He was wearing fishing waders and carrying a fishing pole with a huge lure hanging off it. I looked into his eyes and they were completely vacant. I tried to strike up a conversation and collect the fare but nobody was home. When he got off the train I mentioned to a co-worker that the lure the guy was carrying would never work on the little fish in the river. He laughed and said the guy wasn't fishing. Every week, he'd steal things off the boats in another town and then bring them to this town's pawnshop to hock them. He apparently didn't realize the local pawnshop was closed on Mondays and was just kooky enough to be wearing the stolen waders. He should have listened to a wise old friend of mine who once said, "Don't worry if you have Kleptomania. You can always take something for it".

Just get on the train!

I noticed one passenger vacantly staring at a Smoky

the Bear poster that read "<u>Only You</u> Can Prevent Forest Fires". He gazed back at me and innocently said "That's a lot of pressure on one person".

Just get on the train!

On one steamy afternoon, a frightening looking woman refused to pay her fare. She said, and I quote, "this Bitch ain't paying shit". While we argued, she reached into her pocket, which put me on guard for a possible knife. Instead, she pulled out a card and presented it to me. She actually had a card (which I kept) that said nothing on it except the word "Bitch".

Just get on the train!

One unbelievably scary ex-con always paid his $2.25 fare with a $50.00 or $100.00 dollar bill. Not only did we figure he was using us to launder drug money but he was also depleting us of all our change. After several days of this I decided to give him the business. He handed me a fifty and I gave him back his change as 45 singles, 6 quarters, 2 dimes, a nickel and for good measure, one Susan B. Anthony dollar. He just stood there with steam coming out of his ears, staring at the change and repeating the curse word "f…" over and over. I thought he was going to kill me for breaking his chops but a friend of his told me he was incensed because he wasn't able to count the change and didn't know whether I ripped him off. A few weeks later that same guy boarded my train and took the only available seat, which was right next to me. He was wearing a hooded sweatshirt and something in his pocket kept jabbing into me. I glanced down to see the butt end of a gun sticking out of his pocket. I was very nice to him from then on.

There were times I'd look around a train filled with men, women and children and feel fairly confident that I was the only one on the train that had never been convicted of a felony. Often the train would fill to standing room capacity. One evening we couldn't squeeze the last couple of folks aboard the train. A supervisor agreed to drive the last few folks who were unable to board, to their destination in his car. Pleasant fellow that he was, the supervisor struck up a conversation with the two passengers. He asked why they were heading up north and one responded that he is a drug dealer and the other said he was going to meet with his parole officer. No problem.

SHOT IN THE HEAD

✛✛✛✛✛✛✛✛✛

AFTER A FEW WEEKS OF WORKING ON THIS crazy branch, I was looking forward to working some weekend overtime on a mainline train. When the crew dispatcher called and told me I was instead heading back to the branch, I couldn't believe it. It was a horrendous night due to a tropical storm. Trees and debris were blowing across the highway and my wife couldn't believe I was going back into work. To complicate matters, train service was temporarily replaced with buses due to downed trees on the tracks. The bus that night had very plush seats but the interior lights didn't work and the driver couldn't shut off the heat. Between the rain, the darkness and the heat, the environment was exhausting. Regardless, my band of misfit passengers and I boarded the bus and headed off into the storm. By the time I made it to the last leg of my trip I was soaking wet, overheated, and exhausted. I was so shot, that I stood out in the rain and wind and collected the tickets as the passengers, many of whom were junkies, boarded the bus. A woman about 25 years my junior walked up to the bus. She was having a bad hair day. Bad, like she was just electrocuted. However, she had a smoking hot body, incredible breasts and was wearing a soaking wet, white tee shirt and no bra. I think my head spun around a few times when she tried to hand me her ticket. I don't think it was intentional, but I didn't take her ticket and said, "Just get on the bus" while I probably grinned like a pre-teenager. She apparently thought my not taking her ticket meant that I was making a play for her. I was just seriously distracted. She sat across from me on the bus and started making googly eyes at me. Her body was incredible and I'm pretty sure I'm old so I glanced at my reflection in the window to make sure it was still me. She motioned for me to sit next to her but I kept telling myself, "nothing good can come out of this". Eventually, a big guy boarded and sat down alongside her. She pursed her lips like a kiss and told me I was a fool. After we pulled out (the bus that is), she asked me for a piece of paper. I asked her how big and she said anything so I pulled out a handy dandy seatcheck. She passed it back to me with her name; number and the words "call me". The blood rushed out of my head and headed south and I think I almost fainted as I told myself "nothing good can come out of this". Our last stop was in a fairly bad neighborhood. I avoided the parking lot and left my truck on the street so the bus would pull in right behind my truck. I figured she would be waiting for me when we got off the bus so I kept procrastinating getting off. The longer I waited, the longer she waited, until we were the last two on the bus. Finally she gave up and said goodbye. I watched her standing out in the rain with her broken umbrella and said to myself "Just get in your truck. Nothing good can come out of this". I darted off the bus, and started up my truck. As I sat there, I thought to myself that I knew I loved my wife and wasn't going to do anything. However, the young lady had not only given me her number but was nice enough to prove to me that the old flag could still stand at attention. I knew that nothing good could come out of it but I couldn't just leave her there standing in the rain. Just as I swung the truck around to pick her up, an old, rusted Chevy Chevette, driven by an elderly lady, pulled to the curb and she got in. Whew! Crisis averted.

When I arrived home I was proud as a peacock. I woke up my wife to show her the seatcheck and let her know "I still got it baby"! When I came into work the next morning, my assistant and I had our morning briefing where we'd laugh and try to anticipate what nutty things were in store for us that day. I probably don't have to tell you that I was still strutting like a peacock when I came into work. I showed all my co-workers the seatcheck and started describing the hot chick that was all into me the night before. While I described her, I noticed a weird expression on the face of my assistant. I asked him what was up and he reviewed her looks. Killer body? Check. Awesome boobs, pretty face and incredibly bad hair? Check, Check and Check. With that, he laughed and yelled out "You're talking about Shot in the Head"! I replied, what do you mean shot in the head, like she's a loony tune? He said no, she was nicknamed that by another conductor because she was literally shot in the head. He claimed she was an ice cream man who was shot in the head while selling her wares from her truck. My initial reaction was that you can't be an ice cream "man" if you look that great in a tee-top. I then thought back to an incident where a fellow conductor was robbed at gunpoint on-board his train. The low-life was apprehended when he subsequently robbed an ice cream truck in a nearby town. While not generally considered a dangerous occupation, owning an ice cream truck is apparently not all it's cracked up to be. My assistant conductor continued on that she not only didn't want me, she probably didn't even know what she was doing. That knucklehead took the wind right out of my sails. I lamented about it for a while but eventually got over it. A few years later, I got another call to work overtime on the branch and not only did my little good humor bar board my train, she remembered my name and flirted with me. Shot in the head my ass. She's okay in my book!

Not everyone on this branch line was a few quarters short of a dollar and not all were looks deprived. I met many younger folks who got caught in a web of poverty or drug use and were fighting hard to right their lives. I met a young mom on methadone whose dream was to provide for a better future for her child. A young commuter, who was partially paralyzed from a car accident, fighting addiction and also battling cancer, also inspired me. Despite his problems, he still managed to maintain a positive attitude and took full responsibility for his predicament. And there was a sprinkling of regular, good folks who for whatever reason chose to live in the area and ride the branch despite some of the frightening clientele. In addition, there were my occasional partners in crime, our substitute bus drivers. The conductors on the buses always became close friends with the bus drivers. We deal with the same passenger issues and have much the same stress. One of my favorite bus drivers knew he looked just like Ralph Kramden from The Honeymooners and he played it up completely. He made it a point to dress like Ralphie boy and even sounded like him. He's a great guy who even posed for photos with the passengers.

Another one of our bus drivers referred to herself as "the Diva" and she played the role well. Perfectly coiffed hair, manicured nails and a persona to match her title. One afternoon my replacement bus was loaded with a particularly strange cast of characters when a woman boarded who caused everyone to turn their head. She was older than me but she blew the one to ten scale right out the window. In addition to her overall beauty, she had a low cut blouse on that exhibited much of her ample bosoms. Everyone on the bus took notice. The diva, the junkies, the Cyclops and even yours truly, couldn't miss it. She must have started to get a little uncomfortable because she took a jean jacket out of her luggage and covered up her knockers. When we arrived at the transfer point, I could see she was struggling to handle her luggage while teetering in her killer heels. Gentleman that I am, I offered to give her a hand getting up to the train platform. With that, the Diva burst out laughing as she commented about how genteel I'd be if she didn't have incredible bikini stuffers. Interestingly enough, the beautiful rider just smiled at the Diva's comment. I noticed as we rode up alone in the elevator that in addition to her luggage, she was carrying a fancy looking, long tube. I asked where she was going and she said she was heading to a show in Chicago to sign autographs and the tube contained her posters. I have to premise this by telling you that I've met many famous people at work and my wife doesn't believe any of it. I even ran into actress Kirstie Alley twice and if there weren't witnesses, my bride would still be telling me I'm nuts. That was one of several reasons that I had to ask this gorgeous woman what she did for a living. She replied that she was a makeup artist. I told her that even dumb train conductors know that people don't line up to get autographs from makeup artists so there must be more to the story. Even though there was no one else in the elevator, she leaned close to me and whispered that she was one of the most famous playboy centerfolds in history. She said the first edition she posed in was a top seller because she was the first centerfold to pose nude with her sister. She also said she dated Charlie Sheen in his younger, saner days. I wanted to ask for her photo but since I had already charged her a fare I had nothing to barter so I just let it go. As soon as I got back to the bus I looked her name up on the Internet and sure enough there she was in ALL her glory. I couldn't wait to get home to tell my wife, who needless to say claimed I was full of baloney. A few weeks later, it was a dark and stormy night. The misfits were lined up outside my train when I noticed an older woman that definitely looked familiar. Without the killer heels, low cut blouse and her makeup I barely recognized her but sure enough it was my new friend, the bunny. I cracked open a train door and let her enter, leaving the rest of the riders out in the rain. I excitedly introduced her to my assistant. My goal was to get a photo with her so I could prove to my wife she wasn't another figment of my imagination. Since she makes her money based on her incredible looks, I thought it was very cool of her to allow us to be photographed together without her having on a stitch of makeup. She was an absolutely beautiful woman, both inside and out. She even gave me one of her professional photos. Whether that photo is under my pillow is none of your damn business.

AIN'T LIFE GRAND

⊱┿┿┿┿┿┿┿┿┿┾⊰

Grand Central Terminal

I CONSIDER MYSELF FORTUNATE TO HAVE WORKED out of two of the greatest train stations in the world, New York's Penn Station and Grand Central Terminal. Tragically, the incredibly beautiful, original Penn Station was demolished in 1963 leaving Grand Central as New

York's iconic train terminal. From its majestic towering ceiling and chandeliers to its hidden catacombs it is a place of wonder and mystery. Grand Central Terminal (GCT) is not to be confused with Grand Central Station, which is the name of the adjoining post office as well as the subway station that serves the terminal. Grand Central Terminal was host to several historic railroads including The New York & Harlem Railroad, New York Central Railroad and New York, New Haven & Hartford Railroad. In subsequent years Grand Central Terminal was host to the Penn Central Railroad, Amtrak, Conrail and Metro North Railroad. New York's iconic Long Island Railroad will access Grand Central through their own terminal deep below GCT. New York Central's 20th Century Limited operated into and out of New York from 1902 until 1967. Carnations were given to men and flowers and perfume to boarding women. The train was so popular with the rich and famous that a red carpet was rolled out each time it arrived in GCT. A remnant of that carpet survives in one of Grand Central Terminal's virtually unheard of rooms. In 1937, the President of the New York Central Railroad established a library within the terminal. Today, a non-profit organization, the New York Railroad Enthusiasts maintain an extensive collection of railroad related literature and items including the valuable carpet remnant in the Williamson Library in Grand Central.

Grand Central Terminal was considered a strategic transportation hub during World War II as millions of servicemen and women made their way via GCT to and from the war front. In 1942, four German spies made their way onto Long Island with plans to destroy key logistical northeast locations, including Grand Central Terminal. Fortunately, they were quickly apprehended. In 1944, two German spies were transported by submarine to the east coast of the United States. They landed by raft in Bar Harbor, Maine during a November snowstorm. Having convinced a taxi driver that their car had become disabled, they made their way to Boston so as to catch a train into New York. Their mission was to uncover details about the Manhattan Project through which America sought the atom bomb. They were also instructed to destroy a secret room located ten floors below Grand Central. That room, known as M42, while no longer secret, is still to this day reportedly omitted from the terminal's maps and even from its blueprints. Up until the 1980's various railroads continued to deny the existence of room M42. This strategic area housed rotary converters that converted A/C current to D/C, which was necessary for the operation of the trains. Despite the fact that M42's exact location is still regarded as a bit of a secret, the Germans were well aware of it and were intent on destroying its fragile rotary converters. Soldiers were stationed in M42 throughout the duration of World War II. They reportedly had orders to shoot to kill if a threat presented itself. The two spies charged with this mission were caught prior to succeeding and tried, convicted and imprisoned for espionage.

Visitors to Grand Central Terminal could spend all day perusing the tracks and never find one listed as track

61. This track remains hidden and is rarely if ever utilized. Track 61 allowed for secret train travel from the terminal directly to a hidden underground entrance to the Waldorf Astoria Hotel. Track 61's private platform was first used in 1938 by General John J. Pershing and then in 1944 by President Franklin Roosevelt. For many years a train car on track 61 secretly held Roosevelt's beloved 1933 Pierce-Arrow bulletproof automobile.

Incredibly, Grand Central Terminal was destined for the same fate of demolition as its cousin Penn Station. In the 1980's, Grand Central Terminal was home to more vagrants than many towns. The now elegant Vanderbilt Hall was taken over by an encampment of these unfortunate denizens. In addition, the massive sewer pipes located many levels below the Main Terminal, housed virtual cities of the demented, dangerous and deranged. The nearly three-mile long Park Avenue Tunnel is actually devoid of life, due to the lack of food or clean water and a propensity for getting struck by trains. The terminal however, had no shortage of creatures that joined the homeless in calling Grand Central home. Cockroach-like creatures the size of mice, mice the size of rats and rats the size of cats were the norm. The cats were the size of.... cats, but they were no ordinary housecats. To keep the rodents in check, the since removed feral cats of Grand Central were as tough as they come. When word spread that the city intended to trap and eliminate the cats, good-hearted railroad employees who had fed them for years, set out on a Friday afternoon to capture and save them. They then carted their little friends off to their homes where they intended for them to live out their lives in peace. Those same workers showed up for work Monday morning, covered in scratches and bites as they shared their stories of the destruction and havoc wreaked on their homes by the wild cats of Grand Central. Despite their good intentions, they would have better off attempting to domesticate young jaguars. Not unlike the chickens of Key West or Hemingway's cats, we old-time railroaders miss Grand Central's wild felines who lent an invincible aura to the terminal.

Fortunately, despite the terminal's frightful state, several influential Americans fought against its destruction. They were successfully led by Jacqueline Kennedy Onassis. A plaque stands in her honor in Grand Central Terminal and reads as follows: "In an age where few people sought to preserve the architectural wonders that are a daily reminder of our rich and glorious past, a brave woman rose in protest to save this terminal from demolition. Because of her tireless efforts, it stands today as a monument to those who came before us and built the greatest city known to mankind. Preserving this great landmark is one of her enduring legacies. The people of New York are forever grateful". There's no question that Jacqueline Kennedy Onassis will deservedly, forever remain the first lady of Grand Central Terminal.

SUMMER JOB LASTS 40 YEARS!

‣‣‣‣‣‣‣‣‣

GRAND CENTRAL TERMINAL CAUGHT A MAJOR break because of the dedication of "Jackie O". I caught my big break thanks to "Carole F", who happens to be my sister and who assisted me in getting my first job on the railroad. Like most young boys I enjoyed trains but railroading was never in my career plans. I attended Queensborough Community College in New York but never had any type of career path. I was looking for summer work in 1977 and my sister worked for the New York State Unemployment Agency. She told me she had heard about summer openings with Amtrak's On-Board Services department. If she happens to be reading this and I never thanked her, thank you! I worked that summer as an Amtrak waiter, bartender, coach attendant and sleeping car porter. In my first two jobs on the railroad with Amtrak and Conrail I was one of the few white guys in my department and all of my black co-workers treated me like gold. Despite the racism that was so prevalent towards them they were some of the finest folks I've ever worked with. It was a heck of a job for a kid. I traveled the country and got paid for it. New York's Penn Station to Chicago, Kansas City, Florida, Montreal and more. I worked aboard historic trains like the Montrealer, Kansas City Limited, Broadway Limited and Palmetto. Definitely a dream job for a teenager who enjoyed the lifestyle of being away for days and even weeks on end. The flip side was that the vast majority of my co-workers were divorced due to that same lifestyle and my dog was probably miserable without me. I didn't work that job for long but some memories stayed with me. I'll never forget one incident in Valparaiso, Indiana. Each lavatory had a little sign stating "do not flush toilet while train is in station". There was no retaining tank back then and when you flushed, your poop returned to nature in the form of the track bed. We had stopped in Valparaiso to have a flat wheel checked. As the mechanic crawled under the train, a passenger chose to not abide by the lavatory sign and his business landed directly atop the mechanics head. I bet you could hear him screaming for miles.

After the summer of '77, I returned to college but I had gotten accustomed to earning a paycheck so the poverty lifestyle of a college student no longer seemed appealing. In 1978, I was able to hire on with the

Consolidated Rail Corporation known as Conrail. Conrail was under contract to run the commuter train service in New York and Connecticut. I was assigned as a bartender on Conrail's New Haven Division. At the time there were many bar cars in New York and Connecticut as well as other parts of the country. In addition to handling bar car duties selling alcohol we ran a breakfast car during the morning rush hour period. At night I would operate a bar car from Grand Central Terminal to Connecticut. The railroad would put me up overnight in a very seedy hotel. I still remember being propositioned by a hooker in a sandwich shop near the hotel while she danced and sang to a song called LeFreak by Chic. I rejected her advances but I guess now my wife knows why I get a smile on my face whenever that silly song is played. In the morning I would operate the bar car back to Grand Central selling coffee and danishes. Good times. On more than one occasion I had women take their clothes off and decide to dance for the bar car patrons. For some reason, the combination of booze and trains made people do nutty things. At times, instead of operating on board a train I would be assigned to platform duty in Grand Central Terminal. I would pull a dolly by rope that was loaded up with chests filled with beer, soda and tiny bottles of booze to sell to commuters as they ran for their trains. If a train that was scheduled to have a bar was put in service without a bar car I would drag the dolly aboard the train and sell alcohol, soda and snacks en route to Connecticut.

As many folks know, Connecticut is a very affluent state. What some folks don't know is that it also has some of the most depressed, crime-ridden areas of the country. I often had to detrain at those stops. Once we arrived at our final stop I would have to drag the dolly off the train and make my way over to the opposite platform so as to head back to Grand Central. This was not always as easy as it appeared. At one stop in Connecticut I had to drag the dolly off the train, through the parking lot, through a dark tunnel and then up onto the other platform. That dark Connecticut tunnel represented the first of four times I had a knife pulled on me while working on the railroad. The guy robbed me of a ton of little liquor bottles not to mention beaucoup bucks. The railroad actually demanded I reimburse them for the lost booze. I honestly don't remember how that turned out but I do remember I was pretty shook up and very glad the mugger left me a few Schaefer beers to alleviate my anxiety. The other knife incidents were all while working as a conductor in New York and Connecticut but we'll discuss those later for comic relief.

I COULD HAVE SLEPT WITH
SANDRA BULLOCK

ɪ⊷⊷⊷⊷⊷⊷ɪ

O NE OF THE BENEFITS OF WORKING NIGHTS AND
weekends on commuter trains is what is often referred to as "eye candy". Despite having over 30 years on
the railroad under my belt I was still excited one Saturday
night to be called to work on my scheduled day off out of
Connecticut. The thrill of overtime never faded for me.
As became the norm late in my career, I was the senior
guy working the train but the young engineer and my assistant conductors that evening were funny folks and
great to work with. While collecting fares I ventured into
my young co-worker's car and did a triple-take when I
noticed a young lady. At least she was young to me in that
she was probably mid thirties. It wasn't the beautiful hair

or long, tan, perfect legs that caught my eye first but rather the fact she looked like somebody famous. All right, maybe it was her legs but I digress. More often than not, the passenger turns out to be a star that I either can't name or never heard of. Anyhoo, Little Miss Long Legs and her three good-looking girl friends were enjoying a few adult beverages on their way into the Big Apple. Eventually I couldn't take it anymore and said to her "I know you look like somebody famous but I can't put my finger on it". Her girlfriend raised the ante by replying "I'd bet you'd love to put your finger on it". I let that go and continued on by asking her why I knew her face (I knew her legs too but left that alone). Her knucklehead girlfriend jumped in again and said "you're probably gonna say she looks like Sandra Bullock". I yelled out YES, THAT'S IT! The girlfriend replied, "You're full of baloney and just trying to pick her up". I told her that not only did Miss Long Legs look exactly like Sandra Bullock but that Sandra Bullock is freakin' gorgeous. To say Legs lit up at that comment would be an understatement. She wouldn't leave me alone after that but I eventually retreated back into the cars I was supposed to be working. When our train got into GCT, my young assistant conductor came up to me and said he had a present for me. He then gave me a seatcheck upon which "Sandra" wrote her name and phone number. To this day I almost pass out thinking about it.

Shortly thereafter, I found myself working a regular morning train with a ton of regulars on it. One particular woman made me nuts. Beautiful hair, perfect body and a great personality. With heels she was probably 6'2" so it was only in my mind that I had a shot with her. I should also mention that there was something a little off about her facial features. Attractive but in a weird, strong featured way. Nothing I couldn't live with but certainly no Sandra Bullock. I mentioned to my engineer who also enjoyed the scenery that this passenger looked particularly hot that day in her dress and killer heels. He asked me to point her out and he screamed out "NO WAY!" He went on to tell me that the previous conductor on the train pointed her out too because he was convinced that she was a he! My little nuts refused to believe I was fantasizing about a guy! I told him he was crazy. He then insisted I check out her large Adams apple. He claimed only men have a protruding Adams apple. I couldn't wait till we got to New York to check the Internet to see if he was correct. Apparently not only can women have a noticeable Adams apple but one of the most famous examples listed was Sandra Bullock!

Everyone knows that bartenders and even mail carriers are famous for knowing everyone's personal business. However, conductors are no slouches in that department either. I knew where many of my commuters lived and worked as well as their marital status and other personal information. Much more interesting was the fact that I knew which married passengers were shtupping each other. If spouses knew how many affairs were occurring on my trains, they'd never let their wife or husband leave the house. Every single train had multiple illicit liaisons. One married, extremely hot 40 something year old passenger from upstate New York, blew my mind when she told me she was already a grandmother. I told her she was the hottest grandma I'd ever seen. I came to find out that my mind wasn't the only thing she blew in that she had slept with at least a half dozen commuters on that train alone! Usually these on-board affairs took a little time to develop, but there were exceptions. I had one woman board my train and we hit it off immediately. As we prepared to depart Grand Central, she had to run like a maniac to catch the train. Instead of thanking me for holding it for her, she with great exasperation claimed I had left the station a minute early. I asked her what time she had and she thrusted her cell phone at me. As she did so, the phone's clock changed to 4:30 p.m. We were due out of the station at 4:29 p.m. so I told her we not only hadn't left early, but were in fact one minute late because of her. I was yelling at her but I had a smile on my face so she knew I was just playing. She went on to tell me that she was almost 50 years old and this was her first day on the train after having just returned to the workforce. She mentioned that her wonderful husband would be holding down the fort at home. She boarded my train for the next few days and I couldn't help but notice that each evening one more button was open on her blouse allowing for quite an uplifting view. After just a few evenings she stopped riding my train, which probably put quite a dent in my libido. About two weeks later I happened to work an earlier train and there she was, waiting on the platform looking as fine as ever. She gave me a nice hug as she boarded. I noticed that instead of sitting by herself like she had been, she was squeezed into a two-seater, next to a wealthy, good looking married guy. As I came up behind them to check their monthly passes, I looked down only to see the two of them rubbing each other's inner thighs. Three weeks! She had been only riding three weeks and was already having an affair. I wanted to scream out "Jane, you ignorant slut! Three weeks. You couldn't even wait a month"?

Fortunately, or unfortunately, depending on your perspective, not all our women passengers were quite so loose. One young lady in her twenties asked to speak with me about a guy who was creeping her out. For two days in a row he squeezed into the seat next to her and watched porn on his tablet. He made no effort to keep it out of her view and she was getting pretty uncomfortable. While I'm not sure what he was doing was illegal, I know I'd be upset if she was my wife or daughter. She knew me well so I tried to lighten the mood by saying that at first even I couldn't think of a way for this not to be creepy. Then I told her the only way this would have been funny would have been if she glanced at the porno flick and saw her conductor in the movie! After a few laughs I promised I'd figure out a way to scare him straight. When he boarded I asked to speak with him privately in the vestibule. He knew immediately what was up since apparently he had been doing this for a while in the hope of finding a seatmate that got turned on by his little habit. I gave him the choice of gathering up his belongings and never sitting in that head car again or dealing with the cops at the next stop. I also mentioned that the young lady's father was the railroad's chief of police. Her father was actually a garbage man but why quibble over small details. He tried to tell me it wasn't exactly pornography but related to a poetry site. I kiddingly told him that I'm actually pro-porn, just not on my train! I let him know in no uncertain terms that the only one allowed to be creepy on my train is me. I guess our little talk worked since I never saw anything on his tablet again other than solitaire. I do admit to being a bit of a hypocrite in some of my commuter relationships. Over the years I have had multiple women throw their legs up on a seat and intentionally allow me a birds-eye view of their hoo-ha. My reaction was invariably something to the effect of "Welcome aboard"! But if some guy pulled out his junk on the train I would be screaming for the cops to "Get this pervert out of here"!

Sometimes things are only marginally creepy. Many engineers knew exactly which apartment windows to look into as their train traversed various towns and cities. One engineer would make it a point to stop just short of a red signal on his elevated train tracks so as to view a woman as she made her way around her apartment. There is no doubt in my mind that she knew he could see into her apartment as she pranced about in the nude. Even though he was convinced she was an exhibitionist, he couldn't take a chance of blowing it so he would try to sneak up on her with his train. I can't help laughing when I picture seven coaches and an engine tiptoeing down the tracks with its engine on idle and headlights dimmed. Just like the kid's book "The Little Engine That Could". I think I can…. I think I can…. I think I can….

DO NOT HUMP

┝┽┽┽┽┽┽┥

UNBEKNOWNST TO MOST NON-RAILROADERS the job of conductor takes a toll on the body after decades of repetitive motion. Many years ago I had the frightening experience of humping train cars in Selkirk, New York. Non-railroaders love to take photos of the signs on the side of some freight cars that say "DO NOT HUMP". Humping actually meant a freight train would back up to the crest of a long hill or hump and the cars would be cut free of the train often one by one. The brakeman would ride the freight car while it free-fell without the benefit of brakes down the hill while a switchman lined the route. That route usually led to your coupling onto other freight cars. The only thing separating you from death or dismemberment was your ability to manually crank on the hand brake. Crank too fast and you'd stop prior to your target coupling. Crank too slow and it might be your last ride. I spent many a time sailing down the hill, cranking on the handbrake and screaming like a baby. It's no wonder that in years past, train conductors couldn't purchase life insurance from most major insurance companies.

Thankfully passenger conductors don't experience the peril of humping (in the railroad vernacular). However, while electronic ticketing devices have lessened hand strain, punching thousands of tickets per day remains a leading cause of carpal tunnel syndrome. Solar powered switches are uncommon and most switches are still thrown by hand, literally requiring the shoving of hundreds of pounds of rail side to side. In addition, applying handbrakes to most of our train equipment puts tremendous strain on the back. I'm cognizant of the fact that readers would have to experience putting on a hand brake to appreciate the back strain but you'll have to take my word for it. Knee and hip replacement are extremely common for conductors due to the strain of maintaining your balance on the moving equipment. Over the years I've injured my back more times than I can recall and even herniated a disc in my neck having been thrown forward into a vestibule when the train's emergency brakes were applied.

Also rough on the knees and hips are the recent innovation of high-speed crossovers. These switches allow the train to switch tracks without slowing down. Sounds great except when you're standing in an aisle and not holding on for dear life. I often laugh about the fact that I've fallen into passengers more times than I could count yet I rarely if ever fell into the arms of a beautiful woman. More often than not I ended up sitting on top of some stockbroker named Sidney or Ralph. I recall taking the ticket of a passenger to my right when the train hit a high-speed crossover lurching the equipment to my left. My body uncontrollably spun to the left leaving me facing a very attractive younger woman. I blushed at my lack of grace but said to her "not bad, I almost did a pirouette". The guy across from her blurted out "pirouette my ass, you almost did a lap dance". With that, my regular passengers started pulling out singles. Working the pole baby!

While on the short but sweet subject of freight trains, I was on a 100 plus car freight train on the Hudson that had a car derail back deep in the train. We dragged that car about five miles from Cold Spring, New York to Beacon, New York tearing up five miles of track and shutting down the morning rush hour into Grand Central Terminal. It was my second week on the job and I thought I was going to be fired. I felt bad for the conductor since he was in charge and let me ride up in the engine with him since I was new and wanted to learn from him. If I were in the hack (the caboose) where I'd normally have been, I would have stopped the train when we derailed. There was a brakeman in the hack but for reasons I won't disclose here he was unaware of what was happening even though the ballast was putting dings in the side of the caboose. For you railroad buffs, it was a hot journal box, which is supposed to keep the axles from overheating that failed and caused the derailment. I wish we had camera phones back then because it was a heck of a photo opportunity.

I thought my freight train story about my early days on the job was a winner until a co-worker shared his tale with me. Back then we had majestic old engines such as FL9's. They were cool looking and real workhorses. This brakeman (conductor's assistant) was told by the engineer to climb up the engine's ladder and board the locomotive. Apparently he climbed up the wrong ladder, which was the one that led up the front nose of the engine. The engineer thinking he was on board asked him to pass him his lunch bag. After two or three times with no response, the engineer heard screaming coming from outside the engine. The engineer thinking he was on board, had taken off down the track with the conductor pinned in fright to the nose of the engine. Makes a great visual if you use your imagination!

One of our train yards was unusual in that its yard crew consisted of an engineer, conductor and two brakemen instead of one. The second brakeman was an Indian chap by the name of Abu. Abu was the most polite, efficient and gentlemanly brakeman on the railroad. His radio transmissions were impeccable despite his heavy Indian accent. He was also imaginary. For the longest time, the conductor on the yard job would bark out fake instructions to his fictional brakeman Abu. Despite being Italian, he would reply back in an Indian voice. Countless rail employees looked forward to one day meeting Abu only to eventually realize they had just as much chance of meeting Casper the Ghost.

Another freight tale was told of a crew that operated a freight train switcher on New York's Beacon and Maybrook section of the railroad many years ago. They apparently had a habit of imbibing and would stop and skinny-dip in one of the reservoirs in upstate New York. Upon arriving back in Connecticut the engineer hopped off the engine and ran across the street into the diner. The patrons and workers screamed in horror. Apparently he was so inebriated that he forgot to put his clothes back on. Somehow he drove the train back to Connecticut buck-naked and was so blitzed he didn't notice that he had jumped off in his birthday suit. Thanks to drug and alcohol testing those days are over but they still talk about it in that diner. Having started on the railroad in the 70's during the period of free love and cheap drugs I could certainly relate to that alcohol influenced event. I have intentionally omitted many of the tales from that period because for some reason my recollection is somewhat hazy. More importantly, I am hesitant to share those stories lest readers think drug use is still prevalent in our industry when in fact it is now as close to non-existent as possible.

One of the more interesting locations I worked was on the elevated freight lines near 72nd St. in Manhattan. These tracks would eventually be put out of service only to be refurbished many years later into a park now known as Manhattan's High Line. We would actually back the train right into the second floor of the warehouses and factories on the elevated tracks, where we would couple and uncouple the necessary boxcars. As a young and inexperienced lad, I was amazed looking down onto rooftops only to see tons of naked men sunning themselves and occasionally riding the old rump roast. I didn't realize it was a gay neighborhood and don't know whether I would have recognized the irony in that the neighborhood was and still is known as the "Meatpacking District".

While the elevated 72nd Street line may have left something to be desired, our scenic Hudson line is one of the most beautiful rail lines in the world and is featured on this book's cover. Anyone who likes trains or loves nature should add a trip on the Hudson line to their bucket list. If you ever find yourself in the New York City area, pick up an affordable Metro North ticket from Grand Central to Poughkeepsie. You'll travel the east shore of the Hudson River, passing the Tappan Zee, Bear Mountain and Newburgh Beacon Bridges. Sights of interest include views of the Palisades, Yankee Stadium, Sing Sing Correctional Facility, Indian Point Nuclear Power Plant, Storm King Mountain and West Point Military Academy. Upon arrival in Poughkeepsie you will be just a few blocks from the Walkway over the Hudson, which is the longest footbridge in the world at 1.28 miles in length. The walkway, which soars 212 feet above the

Hudson, was originally the Poughkeepsie/Highland railroad bridge. It was completed in 1889 and in service until decimated by fire in 1974. Rebuilt and reopened as a scenic walkway, it's a sight not to be missed.

LIGHT AT THE END OF
THE TUNNEL

|-+-+-+-+-+-+-+-|

BACK IN THE '70'S GETTING ON TO THE RAILROAD wasn't all that difficult. Getting transferred to a better department however wasn't so easy. One of the first female conductors on Conrail had a penchant for hanging out in my bar car to show me her assets. By assets I mean her paycheck, which was definitely more impressive than mine as a bartender. That put the thought in my head to try to transfer to conductor. In addition, the cigarette smoke in the bar cars was literally making me sick. Another bartender, whose nickname was Shady, talked me into taking the test for assistant conductor. As a disclaimer I have to mention that Shady actually wasn't shady, it just rhymed with his name. Over the years he became one of my closest friends. Shady took the test first and gave me a general idea what I needed to prepare for. He was and is a great guy. He caught the garter at my 1986 wedding and I was thrilled to have him attend my daughter's wedding almost twenty-six years later. Thanks to Shady I aced the test and was eventually transferred from bartender to Assistant Conductor.

WORK RELEASE

‡‡‡‡‡‡‡‡‡

BACK IN THE DAY, ASSISTANT CONDUCTORS RE-ferred to as trainmen or brakemen, were taught to rely on the more experienced conductor when involved in passenger confrontations. I was a total newbie back in the early 80's working a train with a four-person crew that included a conductor and engineer, plus myself and an-other assistant conductor. I was collecting fares near the other assistant conductor when I heard a passenger screaming and cursing at him. "I'll have you fired", I'll have your job", etc. I walked by him and he was actually already writing out the complaint letter and asking me where to mail it. I didn't know what to do so I walked back and told the conductor what was happening up front. This particular conductor was one of the funniest guys on the railroad. It didn't hurt that he looked and sounded just like a famous comedian named Jonathan Winters. I told him what happened and he told me "don't worry. I'll take care of everything". I asked him how and he said, "Just watch". He was downright fat, but waddled his way up the aisle to the passenger who was still steaming. With his nasally voice and eyes filled with fake fear, he asked the guy whether he was the one who had the argument with the Assistant Conductor. The commuter started to go off again but the conductor told him to be quiet and slide over. He squished his fat butt into the seat, squeezing the commuter against the window and told him "we're not Conrail anymore, we're Metro North now". The commuter tried to tell him he couldn't care less but he went on that because "we're now a State Agency we have to hire people on work release and that his assistant was convicted of manslaughter. If you rile him up I don't know what he'll do". He seemed so frantic; that he actually had the commuter believing his assistant was a murderer who at the least would beat the crap out of him. The conductor waited until the assistant started heading their way and told the guy "here he comes. I gotta go. I don't want him to see me with you cause I don't know what he'll do!" The passenger jumped up out of his seat and started apologizing like a lunatic to the assistant who had no idea what was going on. He not only ripped up the complaint letter but offered to buy him a beer when we got to New York. When we arrived in Grand Central he not only bought the assistant a beer from the railroad bartender, he bought me one too! The assistant conductor's expression was priceless as the commuter, sweating in fear, sped away. He had no idea what the conductor told this guy and couldn't figure out what just happened. I wonder if it ever dawned on that commuter that the whole story was baloney.

Surprisingly, that's not my only experience with work release. Unfortunately when the railroad is shut down due to "police activity" it's often code for a person having been struck by a train. One night in the Bronx, we were told that there was police activity in front of us and we'd be delayed indefinitely. If the person somehow survives the incident, they are rushed away in an ambulance and the train continues its journey. Unfortunately, for both the individual and train passengers, if it results in a fatality the train is stuck there until the arrival of a coroner. About a half hour into the delay, a scary looking guy came up to me and demanded I open a window so he could climb out. I told him he was nuts and there's no way I was getting fired if he hurt or killed himself. I asked him why he was flipping out and he said he was on work release and if he didn't report back to the prison on time he was toast. He made it very clear that I either let him out or he was going to find a way to bust out of the train. I discreetly opened a window and he scampered out the window and somehow scaled a twenty-foot abutment. As he ran off down the street, I yelled out, "Thanks for riding Metro North"!

MY HOMOSEXUAL YEARS
(sort of)

NOT SURPRISINGLY, THE TWO BEST PARTS OF working for the railroad were the money and the pretty women. Not much of a shock when you consider I often averaged 70 hours of work a week which resulted in pretty good sheckles, plus I may have been a bit of a flirt. I kind of preferred the term "faithful degenerate" but that's just me. Schmoozing with the ladies not only made the day go faster but it also kept my libido in high drive which was a bonus in light of my wife being younger than me. I would banter with a lady passenger right up to some invisible limit at which time I'd get a little nervous and either stop or run away. Sometimes that limit took minutes of conversation, sometimes weeks. The funny thing is that while I just liked to kid around, I often forgot that there are plenty of women who are actually interested in going all the way which I certainly wasn't. One night I had (and I use the word "had" loosely), a beautiful blonde take a liking to me. She was blessed with pearly white teeth, incredible blue eyes and a body to die for. Married, three kids, late thirties, a nanny and big house in a rich neighborhood plus a condo in Manhattan that she let me know she stayed in alone at least once a week. She would knock down quite a few drinks on the ride home and the beer goggles would kick in making me quite the fox. One night I passed her seat while whistling a tune. For some reason the tune of the day was the Stylistics', "You Make Me Feel Brand New". She asked me the name of the song and I told her, "You make me feel brand new". She said she never heard of it and could I sing a few bars. Ham that I am, I lit right up into "You make me feel brand new... cause God made me for you.... make me feel brand new". She almost leaped out of her seat to tell me that she knew that I was whistling that love song for her. Between her constant flirting, pheromone overload and, oh yeah, the fishnet stockings and see through sweater, my blood pressure was through the roof. Just so happens she was sitting near the vestibule and another passenger overheard our conversation and chimed in that he knew the Stylistics' and had actually seen them twice. The little vixen asked him what year and he said the early 80's at which point she jokingly said, "no wonder I don't know them, I'd have to ask my parents". At that point a passenger in front of her spoke up that he knew them too. She asked him his age and he said late 40's. He was a real nice guy. Actually he was the equivalent of three nice guys. Large black gentleman, about six foot nine and 400 pounds! He said to me that he loved that song and the way I was crooning it. I told him thanks, but it's not really made to be sung by a short Jew. More the style for a black guy with soul. I asked him to try it and I gotta tell you, he was great. She jumped up, pressed herself against me and tried to get me to dance with her in the vestibule. "Mr. Faithful" knew nothing good was gonna come out of this so I told her I wanted to dance with somebody else. She asked who, at which point I proceeded to try to wrap my little arms around the massive black guy. Fifty five years old and there I am dancing in the vestibule with a black guy who could pass for a New York Giants offensive lineman just so I could keep my record of faithfulness intact. Oh and did I mention that I had a raging boner at the time thanks to cutie pie? Dancing with a big black guy while having an erection wasn't exactly on my bucket list. After fifty-five years I definitely not only know which team I play for but I have a no trade clause in my contract! I guess what happens in the vestibule stays in the vestibule. Unless you write a book.

As if that wasn't enough, guess who boards my train the next morning... the offensive lineman. Ironic in that I had never seen him on any of my trains before. Anyways we caught each other's eye, I smiled, he smiled and we chit chatted about the previous night having been pretty funny. I then thanked him for saving my marriage by dancing with me and then I checked. No Boner! Thank goodness.

I'm fortunate to have many friends who play for the other team and I have nothing but respect for them. However, for some reason, getting rear-ended (in accidents) seems to be a regular occurrence with me. Despite more than one train collision, the kookiest collision actually involved my car. My bride and I were sitting at a red light at a very quiet intersection. Not a cloud in the sky or car in sight. Out of nowhere, a Ford Explorer who apparently never touched his brake pedal rocked us from the rear. My wife teared up at which point I realized I didn't have a cell phone to call 911. I ran to the guy behind us and asked for his phone. He wouldn't look at me but finally handed me his phone while shielding his face. His cell phone was ancient and wouldn't connect. After a few choice words I tossed it through his driver's side window at which point he looked up at and said "you didn't have to throw it at me". I was a little taken aback by the bright red schmear of lipstick running up the side of his face. The schnook was a retired judge in his seventies who was wearing a mini-skirt. Instead of noticing me stopped at the light, he was looking in the rear-view mirror applying his lipstick. As my wife was loaded into the ambulance to have her neck checked out, the EMT saw she was crying and asked whether she needed something for the pain. She replied that she wasn't crying because of the pain.

She was crying because she was the only one who didn't get a chance to see what the guy looked like in the dress. At the deposition I was asked whether I was able to "have relations"? I asked the attorney whether he meant by myself or with someone else. I think that comment as well as my testifying as to the color of my nemesis's lipstick prompted a quick settlement on the part of the mini-skirt wearing judge.

Very early in my career, I worked the Harlem line in New York. One of the regular commuters was an impeccably dressed old guy who boarded at an affluent station and who was obviously, flamboyantly gay. Ironically, like my lipstick schmeared rear-ender, this dapper fellow claimed to be a judge. The problem was that I was just a young pup and I wasn't all that comfortable around him. The bigger problem was that no matter how many times I told him to stop, he kept grabbing my butt while I walked down the aisle collecting tickets. Life must have been brutal for airline stewardesses in the old days. It finally reached the point where I snapped and hit him. It was an open handed slap but it almost knocked him out of his seat. He ended up running off in tears at the next stop and made it a point to never ride my train again. In retrospect, I might have been better off simply hanging an "Exit Only" sign on my fanny.

I only bring this story up because it's amazing how your attitude can change as you mature. As a young conductor, I whacked the guy for coming on to me. Fast forward thirty years and you'd see me as a conductor with a heart shaped punch and pink seatchecks, working a train loaded with folks going to the gay pride day parade. I'm sashaying down the aisle and can't believe nobody even notices me! I may be straight, but now any attention is good attention! What a difference thirty years makes.

One of my favorite commuters late in my career was a round, jolly and extremely funny clothing designer named Michael. He had a running routine whereby he kept telling me he wanted to sleep with me even though he was over seventy years old and married to a great guy. I told him that regardless of how funny he was, there was no way I was switching teams after fifty years. He kiddingly offered me a bottle of bourbon for the holidays if I'd play "hide the sausage" with him. I told him make it Woodford Reserve and I'd cuddle but no spooning. The funny fruitcake knew I was kidding but still delivered on the bourbon (and no, we never cuddled).

I LOVE LUCY

╟┼┼┼┼┼┼┼╢

MY EXPERIENCES WITH THE PRIVILEGED BOTH for the better and worse started way back during my first weeks as a young lad working on Amtrak. One of my first assignments on Amtrak was as a club car attendant on one of the first class Metroliner coaches and involved one of the most famous divas of the 70's. This particular coach had just a few dozen swiveling captains chairs and the passengers paid big bucks for a seat. The diva, who was a famous singer, felt it was okay to have her stocking feet up on the armrest of the schlub in front of her. When he asked her to remove her feet, she replied with a line that will live in infamy. "Don't you know who I am"! I didn't do it but I was awfully tempted to make a PA announcement saying that we have a passenger who doesn't know who she is and can someone help us out. In this case I had no idea who she was and I'm not sure whether the other passenger knew either. More importantly, the conductor didn't know who she was and threw her off, kicking and screaming in Philadelphia. Apparently she did know who she was since she made sure she let us know as she was being ushered off the train. The last thing I heard was her threatening to sue us all but I never heard anything else about it. I still laugh when I hear her songs.

Some of my favorite comebacks were directed towards the passengers who thought they were better than everyone else because of their social standing. I've been berated and verbally abused only to reply, "I didn't go to community college for three weeks just to put up with your bullshit". Several times, a rich snooty passenger would argue over a minimal fare only to have me embarrass the money out of them in front of their neighbors by loudly saying, "If three dollars is a hardship for you sir, I'll be happy to waive the fare".

When a passenger would completely lose it, I had a co-worker who would try to keep his cool by responding, "I sense you're upset" or "How's that therapy working out for you"? Those lines never seemed to go over well with the passenger but their fellow riders always got a good laugh out of it.

One can only imagine the number of celebrities a train conductor in a major metropolis would encounter over a nearly forty-year career. One would have to imagine, since

I can't recall or never recognized the majority of them. Other conductors are always reporting star sightings but even when pointed out to me I usually either don't recognize them or never heard of them. Who has time to go to the movies when you're working seven days a week? Despite my lack of celebrity familiarity, a few famous folks left an indelible mark on me. In addition to the folks that have or will be mentioned in these anecdotes, including Pervez Musharraf, a former Miss Florida, the faux Sandra Bullock and a Diva that will remain nameless, there were several other cordial stars on board my trains.

Many of the stars I encountered were not actually on my trains. Instead, I met them while they shot movie scenes in Grand Central Terminal. A few of the movies filmed in Grand Central include: Around the World in 80 Days, Arthur, The Avengers, The Cotton Club, Eternal Sunshine of the Spotless Mind, Gossip Girl, I Am Legend, Madagascar, Men in Black, Midnight Run, North by Northwest, Superman: The Movie and Little Nicky. I mention Little Nicky because the actor/comedian in the lead role was undoubtedly the nicest male star I've ever met. Adam Sandler would spend hours after the day's shooting, schmoozing and meeting with anyone and everyone who reached out to him. He would spend extra time with children and was just an overall great guy.

Lucille Ball filmed a movie in our terminal called "Stone Pillow". As a railroad employee, I was able to gain a little extra access to the actors. During a break in shooting I introduced myself to her. I was taken aback by how nasty she was which seemed to run contrary to everything I had heard about her. When shooting resumed, I mentioned to one of the extras that she seemed like a real bitch. He laughed and said she's a professional who doesn't break character during filming. She was playing a miserable homeless woman and that's who I had met, not Lucille Ball. Interestingly, Lucy insisted that the name of the woman she was playing be Florabelle in honor of her own grandmother. I guess Lucy was very nice but Florabelle (the homeless lady, not Lucy's grandma) was pretty miserable.

I mentioned that the nicest male star I'd met was Adam Sandler. Ironically, the nicest female actress I ever met aboard one of my trains was Lucie Arnaz, the daughter of Lucille Ball and Desi Arnaz. Lucie Arnaz was starring in a Broadway show and was regularly commuting on my train to her performances. It was immediately apparent that she was a genuine down to earth person. She often rode with her young daughter who was a sweetheart as well. Obviously Lucy was a good woman to have raised nice folks like her daughter Lucie and granddaughter.

One afternoon I was walking through the terminal with my engineer and passed two women who were wearing trench coats and leaning against an escalator. I said to my buddy, "those two girls are naked under those coats. He laughed and said I was nuts. We grabbed a bite to eat and headed to our train. As we approached we saw quite a commotion. Passengers were jumping on and off the train while a few guys had video cameras rolling. It turned out I was correct and those two ladies were nearly naked with just a few pasties in strategic areas. They were grabbing executive's ties and rubbing them on their crotch and even tried to pull me into the scene. It turned out that MTV was fairly new and had chosen my train as a prop for a risqué music video by George Michaels. There's never a dull moment in the most famous train terminal in the world.

There was never a shortage of politicians in the terminal at election time including Bill and Hillary Clinton, Jimmy Carter, and a host of governors and mayors. A few politicians that rode aboard my train stood out because of their friendly, natural demeanor. They included New York Mayor Ed Koch, Connecticut Congressman Christopher Shays and former first lady Jacqueline Kennedy Onassis. I even developed friendships with the Ambassadors from both China and Chile who were both commuters.

A few other folks come to mind since they were so nice to our train crews. Al Roker was just as nice to us when he became a bigshot on the Today Show as he was when he was just starting out as a weekend weatherman. The late author George Plimpton always went out of his way to be cordial, as did boxing writer and sports historian Burt Sugar.

Our trains carried plenty of sports stars including New York Ranger stars Mark Messier and Mike Richter. A regular rider who is as nice in real life as he appears on television is former New York Yankee manager and Baseball Hall of Fame member Joe Torre. My all-time favorite train riding sports star is Kara Wolters of UConn Husky fame. Despite being one of the few folks in history to win an NCAA championship, a WNBA championship and an Olympic Gold Medal, she is a very humble athlete and a very nice woman. She is tough to miss on a train since she stands 6'7" but the first time she boarded I naturally couldn't place the face. Once I realized she was from UConn I couldn't help striking up a conversation with her and her husband. When he pointed out her trifecta of championships I told him how lucky he was to sleep with her. He's a few inches shorter than her yet way taller than me, so I'm pleased to report that he could take a joke. I even asked him if he'd mind taking a photo of his beautiful wife and a midget conductor (that would be me) and he happily obliged. Very nice folks.

Basketball Great Kara Wolters and a Shrimp

NO HABLO INGLES

꘎꘎꘎꘎꘎꘎꘎꘎

SOMETIMES, DESPITE MY SPARKLING ATTITUDE, things would occasionally go in the proverbial crapper with a passenger. If it seemed like things were leading up to that infamous line "What's your name? I'm writing a letter", I'd try to discreetly remove my Paul H nametag and replace it with the emergency backup. An engineer friend of mine had used a tool to engrave a little line into the P changing it to Raul H. A supervisor only questioned me one time and fortunately she wasn't the brightest bulb in the chandelier. As she yelled that my name isn't Raul I told her that I'm a Sephardic Jew and would complain to the workplace diversity department if she didn't back off. She had no clue what I was talking about so she just slinked off to find another victim.

Many of the Hispanic folks who rode my trains got a kick out of the Raul H nametag, though a few of them failed to get the memo that it was a fake name. Some, including the Ambassador to Chile would speak Spanish to me only to realize that I didn't understand a word. Riders would often endear themselves to our crews by giving us their newspaper when they were done reading it. I didn't have the heart to tell one migrant worker that even though I appreciated the gesture, I could do nothing but look at the photos in El Diario.

It was amazing how many times I heard the phrase "No Hablo Ingles" when a passenger from a Spanish speaking country owed me money for a fare. It was even more amazing how fast they hablo'd in English if I lied to them and told them they were on the wrong train or shorted them their change. All of a sudden they'd hablo like they were born in the USA. Probably the only time I've been stumped while trying to collect a fare involved a Spanish-speaking passenger who couldn't hablo ingles and who was also blind. The few other passengers aboard the train didn't speak Spanish either so I just wrote that one off as a loss. A blind passenger once threw me for a loss for an answer when he asked me why conductors, when they realize he's blind, always raise their voice when talking to him. He said he always managed to refrain from yelling back, "I'm blind, not deaf, you knucklehead".

In a perfect train world, a conductor would finish his run in the same crewbase where he started, jump in his car and head home. Unfortunately, that's not always the case.

Sometimes there are no trains available to take you back so you have to seek alternative transportation. For Father's Day, as a diversion for my commuting time, my family bought me my first music IPod. The divergence of my never having used an IPod and my having ended my run in a Hispanic, immigrant neighborhood caused quite a scene. The only way back to my car was to hop a bus over the border in the next state. I boarded what I believed was the correct bus and asked the driver to be sure. She looked me up and down and seeing my uniform gave me the old "No Hablo Ingles". I knew she wouldn't have been hired if she couldn't speak English but since I was the only cracker on the bus she probably figured she would give me the business. At best, all of the other passengers spoke broken English so there was no sense striking up a conversation. As they eyeballed me with a look that said I had no business being there, I realized we weren't in Kansas anymore. I started getting a little uncomfortable so I made my way to the back of the bus. This seemed like the perfect time to break out the IPod and find my own private world to hang out in. I put in my ear buds and cranked up some hard rock by Deep Purple. No one else could hear the music but it did a fine job of screening out their conversations, which I couldn't translate anyway. My fellow riders stared me down while we rode through a few fairly dangerous neighborhoods. My nerves were starting to affect my stomach leading to a little gas. Next thing you know, the SBD's kicked in. Silent but deadly, toxic fart time. While Smoke on the Water blared in my ears, I lifted my butt cheek and silently let one go pfffft. The more they glared at me, the more I released SBD's. I figured since they were silent, the other riders would think one of their brothers had one too many burritos the night before. I was relieved when we got to my stop. As I got off the bus the other riders were yelling at me in Spanish but I had no clue what they were saying. I was just glad to be off the bus and away from them. I couldn't figure out why they seemed so upset about having a gringo on the bus. As I walked alone the few blocks back to the train station, I turned off my IPod and removed the ear buds. As I walked, I felt another SBD coming on. I let it go and much to my surprise instead of a silent pfffft I heard a loud BWAPPP! There was no silence there. I walked a little farther and the same thing happened. BWAPPP! I farted so loud a squirrel almost fell out of a tree. I almost fainted when I realized the farts I was releasing on the bus were anything but silent. I was farting my brains out on the bus but the IPod was drowning out the noise making me think they were silent but deadlies. There I was, lifting my butt cheeks and farting like a mental case while the immigrants on the bus cursed at me and thought I was nuts. If I weren't in a uniform that vaguely resembled an Immigration and Customs cop I probably would have been thrown off the bus headfirst. Who knew buying an IPod and not being bilingual could cause your day to stink.

A RECIPE FOR DISASTER

SEAT CHECKS ARE THE LITTLE TICKET STUBS USED
by conductors to designate a passengers designation
as well as whether they've paid their fare. Few things fire
up a conductor more than a passenger grabbing someone
else's seat check in an effort to evade paying for their ride.
We might let dozens of fares go unpaid while chasing
down one seat check scofflaw. I guess it's a matter of
pride. The color of seat checks varies and the system occasionally changes in an effort to keep unscrupulous passengers on their toes. One incident had me feeling like I
was in the Twilight Zone. This particular rush hour train
was so busy that we didn't use seat checks and instead
eyeballed and memorized the passengers as they boarded
so we could collect their fares later. For weeks a beautiful

woman boarded. You couldn't miss her due to her long red hair. I also noticed that she always wore the same jacket every day. She should have been the easiest fare to find but I could never locate her and she kept riding for free. I almost had a heart attack when a regular passenger asked me what's up with the broad who boards at the transfer point? He stated that as soon as she sits down, she changes her coat and pulls off a red wig to reveal her brunette hair. When I walked up to her and charged her I thought she might pass out since she had probably been getting away with her scam forever. She immediately stopped riding my train and is still probably playing her game elsewhere.

A common method to beat the fare was to hide in the bathroom. We had a conductor who went by the nickname of Elvis. He really didn't look like Elvis despite his long, black sideburns but he sure sang like him. In addition to impersonating The King, Elvis became adept at out-smarting the fare beaters. He developed a way to barricade the bathroom door from the outside thereby ensuring a fare beater hiding in the loo would miss his stop. Elvis even carried a little vial of fox urine with him that would normally be used for hunting. If the guy in the bathroom gave him a particularly hard time he would barricade the door and spray the stinky stuff under the door sill. That usually kept them from coming back.

Passengers' hiding in bathrooms was especially prevalent on one of my morning trains. As I swept through the train car collecting tickets I would look for the illuminated "occupied" sign on the restroom, knowing I now had to find a way to get the fare beater out of the john before the next stop where he would in all likelihood jump off. As I passed the restroom I was surprised to see the occupied light was unlit, meaning no one was hiding in the loo for a second day in a row. After opening the doors at the next stop, I stepped into the restroom to relieve myself only to see a passenger pressed up against the wall. I asked him what the heck he was doing and he aggressively said, "I'm all done here" as he brushed past me and took a seat. After taking care of my personal business I exited the restroom, walked up to the passenger and said, "tickets please". His response was a loud "the ticket thing is over motherf....."! I said, "what" and he replied, "the ticket thing is done and you already took the tickets"! I took off my hat, looked at the conductor badge and said, "I'm the conductor. I decide when the ticket thing is over. Now hand over your freakin' ticket". With that, he called me an a-hole and grudgingly gave me a one-way ticket from Westchester to Grand Central. He actually thought he could intimidate me and dictate when I could collect tickets. You can't make this stuff up.

For many years we had a young fellow ride our trains who while not short of all his marbles, definitely had a hole in the bag. Even if he had money he liked to play a game with the conductors, claiming he was broke and needed a free ride. Sometimes the conductor would get annoyed but more often than not he would let him ride because the conductor realized he was a little slower than the norm. To make matters crazier, he even managed to endear himself to a few crews and would beg to no end for a ride home from the station. One day the crew decided to play a little prank on him in an effort to stop his requests for a ride. One of them had a carry permit for a pistol and decided to put a little scare into him, but not in the way you might imagine. On the way to the kid's house, they pulled into a gas station and he filled his truck with fuel. He then jumped back into the car and pulled out his gun. The poor kid almost pooped his pants and asked what was going on. My co-worker told him that he had just robbed the gas station and they had to make their get-away. The kid bought the act hook, line and sinker, was scared to death, and never asked for a ride home again.

Over the years I got into the habit of using seat checks as my filing system. In fact, this book wouldn't have been possible without them. One evening, in an effort to bond with my wife, who I affectionately refer to as Breezy, I scribbled the following words on a seat check. *"Boy did we have great sex last night!"* I handed it to her in front of my daughters; careful so as not to let them read it. I met my goal as I got Breezy to blush profusely and then I mindlessly returned the seat check to my uniform pouch. Needless to say, my first passenger in the morning was a zoftik (full figured) Italian lady in her fifties and she got the magic seat check that I forgot that I had returned to my pouch. The look on her face was a mix between anger and astonishment. It must have taken me ten minutes to explain the story over and over, even offering to have her call my wife before she finally agreed to drop her threat to write a complaint letter. I ended up befriending her and she gave me what turned out to be a great recipe for fettucine alfredo!

Sex, food…. It's all good. Boil the noodles, nuke the shrimp and then just mix it all together.

1 lbs. box of fettucine noodles
16 oz. sour cream
1 1/2 cup grated parmesan cheese
3/4 stick butter
1/3 lbs. honey ham julienned to look like the noodles only pink
1 lbs. cooked jumbo shrimp
black pepper to taste

HORSING AROUND

THERE ARE NO GUARANTEES IN MARRIAGE, BUT I can assure you that if I ever get divorced it won't be because of this book. My wife and I are so close that I've already told her all of my stories, except this one! I wasn't trying to keep a secret. It was just that I figured that if I found it a tad creepy then she would too. I had a lovely, older, married woman ride my train each day. She must have been quite a beauty in her day but she was now a little long in the tooth. She came to me and said she had something to give me but first wanted to share the fact that she had developed some deep feelings for me. I was a little embarrassed as she handed me an envelope, which I stuck in my ticket pouch. I later opened the envelope and inside was a poem she had written about me. I've heard that divorce lawyers cost a bundle, so the poem will never make it into print. I have to tell you that I'm not tall, dark or particularly handsome so I have no idea how or why this stuff happens to train conductors.

Once I got married, there was many a time I found myself running away from potential dalliances. A married, frequent commuter asked me what sounded like "Do you wanna be my boyfriend"? I blushed and gave it the old hamana, hamana, hamana, and then I repeated what I thought she had said. She laughed and replied that she had actually said, "Do you want to SEE my boyfriend"! She then pulled out a photo of her standing alongside her horse so I could see her "boyfriend". We had a good laugh and then she drew me in close and said, "I'm glad you brought up the subject since I've been looking for a way to broach this subject". She then said, "My husband and I have an open marriage". I think my eyeballs might have nearly popped out of my head. Nothing dirty happened because I think I may have fainted.

I have to admit that despite the fact I was faithful, there were a few attractive commuters I let know were in the on-deck circle should something unfortunate happen to my wife. Not that I'm expecting anything nefarious like an industrial accident or brake line failure. However, since the only way I would go out with someone else would be if something terrible happened to her, the worst words my wife could ever hear would be "Now Batting for Lisa Holland, number 24, … …..".

Despite that sexy commuter's horse I've always been

more of a dog lover. However, our railroad has a very liberal dog policy that's been a bone of contention for conductors. No crates or muzzles are required and dogs are allowed on-board with little or no enforceable restrictions. While detraining my passengers down the steps to what was a low level platform, I had a pitbull leap off the top step in what was definitely not an attempt to get a hug. I tore ass and ended up a block away before I knew it. I never let that guy board with his dog again and I've had a fear of pits ever since.

Wackier than killer dogs are the passengers that insist on putting their dog up on the seat. It's a rule violation but good luck enforcing it when the dog is from a rich town in Connecticut and has a trust fund bigger than your 401k. I got into an argument with one snob who refused to take his dog off the seat of a busy train. I told him we would end up with standees and there was no way the dog was going to take up a seat while passengers ended up standing. His argument was that the floor was too dirty and apparently not good enough for Fluffy. I asked how old the dog was and he said five. I calculated five in dog years and told him to either get the dog off the seat or buy the dog an adult ticket for twenty-two bucks or I was calling the cops. Without blinking an eye, he sprang for the twenty-two bucks and I ended up issuing a train ticket to Fluffy. It was pretty uncomfortable telling the standees that I couldn't ask the guy to move his dog because the dog paid his fare. It was amazing I never received a complaint letter on that one.

Probably because of the uniform, we're always being asked to pose for pictures. One day a lady with a double stroller walked over to me and asked if I would allow her to take a photo with her babies. It wasn't until after I leaned in for the photo that I realized her two babies were real mutts! They were two cute little terriers obediently sitting side by side in an infant's double stroller.

We try to keep dogs, and more importantly people's shoes off the seats in an effort to keep the seats clean. I reported for work and noticed that one car's seats looked particularly shiny and clean. I have to assume the railroad was trying out a new cleaning product. That product resulted in what was the funniest candid camera moment I've ever had aboard my trains. We left the yard and stopped at our initial station where a dozen or so passengers boarded that car. As we approached the next station, I happened to be looking down the aisle of the car. The engineer applied the brakes and in unison each and every passenger slipped off their seat and onto the floor. As some yelled and others laughed, I sat down in one of the seats to see what had happened. Upon sitting down, I slipped right off the seat and under the one in front of me. Whatever they were using on those seats turned them into the slipperiest surface I had ever seen. I actually had to close the car down which resulted in standees because the seats were so slick. It was one of the funniest sights I've ever seen.

THAT TIME OF THE MONTH

┣┿┿┿┿┿┿┿┿┫

THE TOUGHEST DAY FOR A CONDUCTOR TO collect fares is the first day of the month. Hundreds of commuters can be counted on to forget to buy their monthly commutation ticket. With rare exception, the conductor is expected to squeeze a one-way fare out of these passengers even though they will eventually buy the monthly pass. Conductors being human (usually) may cut a break for a regular commuter with a reasonable story. On the other hand, the first of the month gives us a chance for payback when it comes to any arrogant, condescending passengers. It's incredible seeing a guy who drives a Maserati hiding in the bathroom because he forgot his monthly and it would kill him to spring for $20.00. How can you not laugh when some rich guy who is used to being waited on hand and foot screams "It's not MY fault I don't have my ticket". It's difficult not to respond back, "Whose fault is it? The conductor, the railroad, your butler, Santa"? My favorite first of the month is January, when passengers try to tell you they didn't realize it's a new month. How the hell can you not notice New Year's Eve? At times I treated the 1st of the month like a game as I tried to get my pound of flesh out of them before letting them off the hook. It's amazing what you can get away with saying as long as you eventually let them get away without paying. I'd often ask them if they ride my train every day. They'd almost always respond yes at which point I ask them if they say hello or good morning to me each day while I make believe I don't recognize them. One morning I went a little overboard with my act before cutting a passenger a break. As soon as I got to the next rider he boomed "Good Morning", as he reached out to shake my hand. Sure enough I looked down in his lap and he only had the prior month's ticket. He was listening in on my act and obviously paying attention. My all-time favorite experience was when a mature woman who was a regular rider boarded with her two grown daughters. She gave me the regular spiel about forgetting her ticket at home and I went into my "I've never seen you before in my life" act. At that point, she threw out her chest and yelled out "C'mon. You don't recognize these big hooters"? I burst out laughing but her daughters were mortified and looked like they wanted to crawl under their seats.

One of my favorite first of the month stories involved a wealthy passenger who claimed he thought he bought his new monthly pass but couldn't find it in his wallet. I told him I get paid by the hour so go ahead and look thoroughly through the wallet before I bang him for the $20. After pulling out what seemed like dozens of cards from his wallet ranging from credit cards to the AAA he admitted he simply didn't realize it was a new month. I burst out laughing when I realized one of his cards was a membership card for MENSA, the high IQ club for geniuses. He was a certified genius so I said to him, "So you're a genius but you have no idea what month it is"? Beautiful, just beautiful.

Speaking of geniuses, it's never a great idea when running down the platform late for a train to repeatedly shout out to the conductor, "I'm Coming! I'm Coming! I'm Coming" without expecting an off-color response.

I SCREAM, YOU SCREAM, WE ALL SCREAM FOR ICE CREAM

⊱━━━━━━━━⊰

ONE OF THE MOST DIFFICULT ASPECTS OF BEING in the service industry on the "Gold Coast" of Connecticut is dealing with both extremes on the socio-economic scale. For many if not most of my co-workers it is far easier to deal with the attitude of the poor than that of the affluent. One of our branch lines is notorious for their holier than thou attitude while another is known for folks down on their luck as well as a few (okay way more than a few) crazies. Right smack in the middle is the branch I usually worked, one of the most desirable runs on the railroad. The wealthy branch's folks are politically connected. Indicative of that is that unlike the other two branch lines, the wealthy branch line's customers pay no more for their ride than passengers boarding down the line at their main line connection point. They ride their branch for free! In the immortal words of legendary comedic writer Mel Brooks, "It's good to be the King!" While the wealthy folks manage to complain despite their riches, the poorest riders make do with the worst equipment and least frequent service. The announcement "Train service has been suspended, bus service will be provided" is a frequent mantra on the less affluent branch line. Despite being the stepsister of the three CT rail branches, the down on their luck folks, for the most part maintain a healthy attitude. However, there's some unknown magic about the branch I worked that keeps commuters happy whether rich or poor. It's probably no surprise that the illegal immigrants are pleasant, pay their fare and keep to themselves. The drug dealers coming to ply their wares on the North end of the branch pay their proper fare and remain reasonably quiet so as not to draw attention to their drugs. Perhaps most surprising is that even the riders boarding at towns where a buttered roll could cost twice as much as dinner in other towns are for the most part, civil, caring and friendly to our train crews. Naturally however, there's always the exception to the rule. All trains seem to take on a personality and every train has its characters. One afternoon train had a grizzled older man who commuted daily to one of the more affluent stops. He was the most miserable, grouchy, chain smoking grump that could be found. I would thank him every day and wish him a wonderful afternoon just to aggravate him. One rainy afternoon, an attractive thirty-something woman boarded with her young daughter, probably around seven years of age. Like many conductors I would often avoid asking passengers to remove their shoed feet from the seats lest I get a verbal smackdown from the hoity toity or a physical smackdown from one of our poorer customers. However, since it was raining I asked the woman to remove her wet shoes from the seat opposite hers. You would have thought I demanded her first born. She proceeded to demand my name, threaten to call my superiors, and belittle me to the point even I was almost impressed. She left me so frazzled that when the old grumpy guy headed for the vestibule when nearing his stop I decided for the first time to engage him in conversation. Bearing in mind that he barely would respond to my years of hellos, what followed was amazing. I proceeded to ask him if he is always this miserable and he responded with a synopsis of his life story. Working as an international stock broker he was forced to take the first mainline train in the morning arriving at his departing station at the ridiculous time of 4:30 a.m. Apparently, appreciating whiskey, chain smoking and awakening at 3:00 in the morning Monday through Friday comprise the perfect recipe for a piss-poor attitude. He went on to state though that the two loves of his life are his wife and the ice cream shop he purchased for her to run. He said that upon entering the ice cream parlor his entire demeanor changed for the better. I was unaware that the woman who had verbally berated me was standing behind us while this conversation carried on. Upon hearing the name of the ice cream shop, she blurted out how she was new to the area and how she and her family absolutely love his ice cream shop and that she's in there all the time. My grumpy buddy who I apparently misjudged to a magnitude that can't be described turned to my tormenter and snarled….. "I DON'T APPRECIATE THE WAY YOU TALKED TO THE CONDUCTOR! DON'T YOU EVER STEP FOOT IN MY ICE CREAM PARLOR AGAIN"!!!! He continued to berate her, stating that you don't treat people that way and she should be ashamed of herself for setting an example like that in front of her young daughter. There probably existed a slight chance that she may have apologized to me but she was way too mortified to comment. The next day when I expressed my thanks to grumpy and let him know what he did was one of the coolest things I ever experienced, I saw him smile for the first time!

9/11

┣╍╍╍╍╍╍╍╍┫

I PROMISE NOT TO STAY SERIOUS FOR LONG, BUT obviously this is a difficult and sensitive topic. September 11, 2001 was rightfully an incredibly emotional day for our entire country. For obvious reasons, New York and its commuters were traumatized from the events that day. In the aftermath of the attacks, our railroad was one of the few available means to get on or off the island of Manhattan. The initial emotional issue for our crews arose from transporting thousands of our regular riders, seemingly in shock, with their suits, dresses and hair engulfed in dust. We spent the ensuing days bringing emergency workers and volunteers into the city. Naturally everyone was on edge. It seemed a bomb threat was called into our stations or trains nearly every day for weeks. The eerie and unprecedented silence from those aboard our trains seemed almost mournful but was a result of the emotional shock of commuters who witnessed the destruction and suffering. The constant ebb and flow of familiar cars in our commuter parking lots stopped. It was heart wrenching to see the cars of our commuters and friends remain in the lots for days and weeks, knowing their owners would never return for them. It seemed everyone bonded together by contributing donations or emotional support to the many families who lost loved ones. Even our railroad's tailor took it upon himself to spend countless hours, hand fashioning black, flag draped armbands for our conductor uniforms. I still have those bands and even all these years later I get emotional looking at them. We not only lost commuters that day but some wonderful friends as well. May they rest in peace.

LAST CHANCE FOR ROMANCE

▸▸▸▸▸▸▸▸◂

IN ADDITION TO BEING A CONDUCTOR, I USUALLY had a side gig of some sort. After approximately fifteen years on the railroad, my co-workers elected me secretary of our union. I was proud that they continued to re-elect me for the remainder of my career. Our union meant a great deal to me since in our industry it is vital to have an entity that demonstrates that they care about your safety and the welfare of your family. Our union office was located in an office building adjacent to Grand Central Terminal. Due to my late hours I was often the last one in the office and I ended up bonding with the cleaning lady. She was the friendliest person you could ever meet. Her only downside was she looked a little like the cousin of the abominable snowman. I believe she was from the Russian Caucasus and she looked like she could wrestle a bear and win. She was taller than me, broader than me, heavier than me and probably hairier than me. While she cleaned the office one evening, we heard a huge explosion and the building seemed to shake. She immediately thought we were under attack and insisted we had to hit the stairwell. Since we were only on the second floor I told her I had to save something on the computer and I'd be right down. When I didn't respond to her repeated calls of "Mr. Paul, we got to go", she panicked and literally lifted me in the air and started carrying me out of the office. I got out of her grip and followed her down the stairs. All she could think of was that we were going to die. All I could think of was that the world might be ending and this hairy cleaning lady would be the last woman I'd ever see or have a shot with. Since you're currently reading this book I have to assume you can probably figure out that it wasn't the end of the world. It turned out to be a Con Edison gas explosion, which took out a large section of Lexington Avenue in Manhattan.

The world changed on September 11th and to a degree we'll now always remain on guard. In the aftermath of attacks on trains in Spain, we learned that the terrorists used cell phones as detonators. One morning, a passenger came up to me with total fear in her eyes. She asked me to call the cops because a passenger of Middle

Eastern descent was sitting in his seat staring at his cell phone. Somehow, that didn't quite rise to the level in my mind of having him arrested. Regardless, I figured I'd ease her concern by checking it out. He had a flip phone open in front of him and he was just holding it there. The weird part was that the phone wasn't turned on. I still didn't feel particularly threatened but I asked my assistant to check him out and give me his opinion. He felt the guy was just a nutjob and not a threat but if we ignored it and something bad happened we'd be toast in more ways than one. I radioed the rail traffic controller and let them know our concerns. They said the police would meet our train a stop or two down the road. When we arrived at the next several stops there were no cops to be seen. This went on until we arrived at one of our bigger stops where the guy got off. At the next major stop I saw a railroad cop running down the platform with a dog. He asked me where the guy was and I told him he already got off. The cop berated me for letting him get off but I told him the dispatcher said the cops would meet us within a few stops, not half an hour later. He wouldn't let us leave the station without his bomb-sniffing dog checking out the car the passenger was in. The dog was a small, cute yellow Labrador retriever. When he and the pooch first entered the bathroom, the dog had a bit of odor overload. Eventually he stuck his head into the toilet and lapped at the blue water. I couldn't believe they taught the dog to sniff out bombs but never taught him not to drink toilet water. The cop seemed embarrassed and headed down the aisle with the pooch. All of a sudden the dog froze in front of a passenger who was coincidently sitting near the guy who had the phone. The dog froze, the lady froze, and the cop went into official police hyper-drive mode. He anticipated the worst, but instead the dog leaned in and started to lick the cream cheese off the lady's bagel. Crisis averted.

IT'S ALL FOREIGN TO ME

┣┿┿┿┿┿┿┿┫

THE LAST TRAIN OF THE DAY DEPARTS GRAND Central after 1:00 a.m. and is unaffectionately referred to as the "Vomit Comet". The two or three trains preceding the comet are loaded with drunks who tend to fight, refuse to pay their fare and perform other vile acts against nature. However, by the time the Vomit Comet rolls around most of the fight is out of the drunks and the difficulty arises when an attempt is made to awaken them for their fare. It is even harder to get them off at their intended stop. Invariably we will find passengers asleep or borderline unconscious at the last stop of the night. In the good old days it was just heave ho and out they went to sleep it off. However, in our newer litigious society for the most part we no longer physically remove the passengers. We now leave that to the police and ambulance crews. One night upon arriving at our final stop I came upon a knocked out, well dressed passenger who still had a half empty bottle of Saki sticking out of his pants. I informed him that the next southbound train would be leaving in about four hours and he should enjoy his stay on the desolate train platform. He then told me he was just promoted to vice-president of his company and had to be at work in the morning. He asked me to drive him home and I told him that A. my car was old and B. my wife was home pregnant so I had no desire to take a twenty-minute detour. He then offered me all the cash in his wallet to get him home. Opening his wallet he then presented seven fifty-dollar bills. Upon arriving home my wife was upset that I was so late but her attitude changed quickly when I split the $350 bucks with her!

Another time I had a young lady miss her connection due to my having given her faulty information. I felt bad so I offered to drive her to her station. Turned out she was starring at the time on Broadway as a feline in the musical CATS which made for some purrfectly stimulating conversations.

But enough of my side-tracking so let's get back to foreigners. One of my angriest foreigners was a German guy visiting relatives in New York. He was screaming like a lunatic when we arrived at our last station stop because he thought that the railroad police removed the wheels from the car he had borrowed from his relatives because he parked without a permit. I couldn't make him understand that because the station was so quiet and isolated it was the number one spot on the system for having cars stolen and broken into. Some lowlife stole the rims and tires off the car but he went back to Germany convinced the cops took his rims to teach him a lesson.

We have a station called North White Plains that is always written as No White Plains. There isn't a conductor on the railroad that hasn't had a "Who's on First" moment with at least one Asian commuter trying to get to No White Plains. No White Plains? Yes White Plains? No White Plains? Yes White Plains! We also stop at a station called Cannondale. I nearly fell down laughing when a gentleman from Japan excitedly mentioned to me that he was amazed at how fast we had made our way to Canada. No matter how hard I tried I couldn't make him understand that "Cannondale" and "Canada" are not one and the same. He must have thought we were on the Bullet Train to have made it from Grand Central to Canada in under two hours.

I had an elderly Asian women who rode my train for a while who would clasp her hands in front of her and repeatedly rant "too fast, too fast, too fast" as we headed down the track. I tried to explain to her that we were going under the speed limit and she needed to stop alarming the other passengers. She wouldn't stop and I started getting angry with her until I realized she was short a few marbles. Her adult son met her at her station, so I took him aside and explained the situation. He, his Mom, and a few other relatives showed up the next night at the station so she could apologize to me and present a cake to ask for my forgiveness. I didn't see her for the next few days and felt guilty that I might have scared her away. A week or two later my assistant mentioned to me that there was a strange older woman sitting up front. I walked up and sure enough, there she was, sitting with her hands clasped in front of her like in prayer, repeating the words "not too fast, not too fast, not too fast".

My favorite tourists were always the camera happy Japanese. There must be a thousand photos of me on Far East mantles. One lovely summer day we arrived at our last stop in upstate New York. Sure enough, a Japanese rider jumped off and immediately started snapping photos of the flora and fauna. Eventually, he walked up to me and in broken English said, "I have no idea, New Jersey so beautiful". I explained to him that he was in New York and not New Jersey but he kept arguing that Dover is in New Jersey and we just passed Paterson, New Jersey. I patiently tried to explain to him that we were in Dover Plains, New York, not Dover, New Jersey and the Patterson we passed had two T's not one. The more belligerent he became the more I lost my patience. Finally I pointed to the mountains he was photographing and told him that they were the foothills of the Berkshires. Not only are the Berkshire Mountains in Massachusetts but you can't see Massachusetts from New Jersey! When I gave up on him he was still yelling at me "You clazy, you clazy"! Okay. You don't what state you're in but I'm the one who's crazy.

While I never got to see the photo, my best shot is undoubtedly someplace in Japan. While my train sat on a platform in Grand Central I took a moment for a nature break. As I stood in the tiny bathroom of one of our older train cars, with my little schmeckler in my hand, I saw light bulbs going off. I knew nobody was in the loo with me so I thought I was cracking up. I then realized that the thin film that was supposed to obscure the bathroom window had peeled off. Lined up on either side of the lavatory window were the wife and kids of a Japanese tourist. Somewhere in Japan is a photo of a mom, two kids and my schmeckler.

Apparently, we have no shortage of Asian riders but I promise this is their last story. My train pulled into a station where only two doors fit on the platform. Our regular commuters were dutifully lined up exactly where we would land the two doors. As we pulled in I jokingly announced that we only had room for four more riders and I pointed to a few of them, winked and said "you, you, you and….. you". Almost everyone else either laughed or gave me the finger but I saw one young Asian lady forlornly walking away. I asked her where she was going and with the saddest face she replied, "you didn't pick me". I guess sometimes my sense of humor just doesn't translate well.

IS THERE A LAWYER IN
THE HOUSE?

├─┼─┼─┼─┼─┼─┼─┤

THE FIRST RUSH HOUR TRAIN OF THE AFTER-
noon is one of the least desirable trains to work.
The reason is that a ton of passengers have cheaper off
peak tickets that have to be stepped up to the higher rush
hour fare. After selling dozens of step-ups I came upon a
women in her forties with a son about ten years old. She
refused to pay me the four-dollar step up because "nobody told her" that the fare is higher in the rush hour. I've
always loved that excuse. Like there's a little train fairy
that runs around and gives out all the tariff rules to each
individual rider. After wasting a ton of time on her she
still refused to pay the four dollars. I realized she had
been drinking when she blurted out "I am not intoxi-

nated". That's not a spelling typo. She really said intoxi-nated. She managed to get my blood pressure so high that I called for the police at 125th street station in Harlem. Naturally when the police arrived she promptly paid me the fare in front of the cops and said the only problem was my attitude. What a piece of drek. Months later I was notified by the railroad that the cockamamie lady filed a notice to sue on the grounds of loss of future earnings of her little kid. She claimed her kid was so traumatized by my actions that he now refused to go into the city for auditions. Apparently she was trying to get him acting auditions and thought he was going to be the next cute little actor. I call bullshit. Hopefully the railroad didn't pay her for her act.

While we're discussing b.s. lawsuits, another comes to mind. More absent-minded folks fall into the gap between the train and platform than people realize. Usually it only results in a nasty scrape or injured knee. I was working a train that had just pulled into a station and I popped open the doors. All of a sudden my female assistant conductor who was prone to getting excited started shrieking on the PA that somebody fell into the gap. I actually witnessed it and couldn't believe my eyes. A skinny kid stepped off the train and dropped out of site into the gap. Fortunately his Dad was one of the few folks smart enough to hold his kid's hand getting off the train. The father treated his kid like a yo-yo. The young kid dropped into the gap and the father held on and sprung him right back up. I ran up but the kid didn't have a scratch and wasn't even crying. Weeks later I was notified that a woman was suing the railroad for the cost of the jewelry and money in the pocketbook she lost on the tracks when she "jumped down to save the poor child". Nobody ever jumped on the tracks and the kid himself didn't even fall that far. She apparently witnessed what happened and came up with her story in the hope of a financial windfall. I sure hope she was told to get lost by the legal department.

HAPPY HOLIDAYS

━━━━━━━━

IT'S THE NATURE OF THE BEAST THAT TRAIN CON-
ductors work on holidays. The trains run on Thanksgiving, Christmas, etc. so we have to be there. Many
people assume that New Year's Eve is the toughest day to
work due to the crazy partying. I never minded New
Year's Eve since the drunks are usually happy drunks.
Other than dealing with projectile vomit and unconscious passengers, it isn't too tough to handle. Parades
present much bigger problems. The Thanksgiving Day
Parade causes the trains to be jammed with families but
once again, everyone is in a good mood so there are few if
any problems. Salute to Israel Parade. Mazel Tov. No
problem. Gay Pride Day Parade. Feel free to dress up (or
down). No problem. St. Patrick's Day and Puerto Rican

Day Parades. Big problems. Sometimes I think St. Patrick must have been the Saint of fighting. Fisticuffs on board the trains are commonplace. The Puerto Rican Day Parade is another winner if you're a big fan of knifings and shootings. Sometimes the two groups mix, with less than spectacular results. One year I was boarding the crowds from the Puerto Rican Day parade with my Hispanic assistant conductor when a few drunken Irish-American guys wobbled down the stairs. They immediately started in about how they hated these dirty Puerto Rican Spic this and dirty Spic that. My assistant remained calm but I completely lost it on his behalf. I called the police and had the drunk Irishmen carted off. Once they were gone, I turned to my assistant and asked how come I was the one so upset in light of the fact that I'm Jewish and he's the Hispanic and he replied "I'm not Puerto Rican, I'm Cuban so it didn't faze me at all". I need to buy a globe. Other big events included Santa-Con and Comic-Con, both of which made for some great passengers. My male colleagues would trip over each other in an effort to work Santa-Con trains. We're talking about the hottest Santa Clauses and elves you could imagine. Comic-Con always had a few incredible Wonder Women but more often included guys like Barf the Mawg from Mel Brooks Spaceballs movie.

JEW ARE YOU?

‡‡‡‡‡‡‡‡‡

IN THE OLD DAYS IT WASN'T DIFFICULT TO BE CON-sidered a minority on the railroad. If you weren't Irish or Italian, you were a minority. I was comfortable working as a bartender with my mostly African-American friends on the rails and actually questioned whether I could be a conductor since I wasn't Irish or Italian and I didn't smoke or play poker. Fortunately I did drink, so at least I met one criteria. As a Jew from New York City, I didn't fit the stereotype for a conductor on the railroad but I figured my having dropped out of Queensborough Community College pretty much ruled out medical school. Irish/Jewish had me thinking I had the ish part right. In fact, for a while I wore a "Kiss Me I'm Irish" button on my uniform coat. When I picked up my future wife on the train, she saw that button and excitedly told her German Mom that she had met a very nice Irish guy on the train. Woops. Getting along with Italians was always a snap. Italians and Jewish families have the same priorities, family, food and guilt. However, to save myself some aggravation, I didn't discuss my being Jewish with my co-workers unless it somehow came up in conversation. I later found out that I wasn't the only one who took that tack. One co-worker was known for many years as "George". He was a gregarious guy who was well liked. One afternoon he accepted an invitation to another conductor's home. He expected an afternoon of drinking and cards. Instead it was a recruitment meeting for the Ku Klux Klan. The other railroaders in attendance weren't aware that "George's" real name was Jorge and he was Puerto Rican, not Italian. George passed on the opportunity to join the Klan. I assume his heritage would have ruled out becoming Grand Dragon anyway.

On more than one occasion I questioned whether I would ever fit in on the railroad. When Metro North was formed to replace Conrail as the operator of passenger train service out of Grand Central, I and a woman conductor I was close with found ourselves laid off by Metro North. Since we were on the same seniority district roster as Amtrak we headed over to Penn Station and became Amtrak conductors from New York to Boston. After collecting fares out of Penn we couldn't find the rest of the crew. We eventually located them playing poker in the baggage car. As we entered the car we witnessed them throwing boxes of newborn chicks off the train because their peeping was apparently disturbing their game. We were mortified as we watched the boxes fall into the water below the Hell Gate Bridge. As if that didn't bother us enough, we realized the crew was using a coffin as their card table. I hope the poor stiff was a card player. While I know those guys weren't indicative of all their conductors, we both made our way back to Metro North as soon as we could.

On my first day as a passenger conductor on Conrail, I drove from Queens, N.Y. to a crew base a hundred miles or more up to the North. I parked next to an old pick up truck and glanced into the bed. In the rear was a bleeding and apparently dead red fox that had been caught in a trap. As a city kid, I was a little taken aback. I then went to the train crew building to sign in and saw a large swastika painted on the side of the concrete edifice. I asked a conductor who appeared older than dirt about it and he said they liked it because it kept "undesirables" away. He then went on to tell me how they had driven a black supervisor out of the crew base by putting a severed pig's head on the hood of his car. At that point on the outside I looked great. On the inside, I wanted to run home to mommy.

The old-timers had unique personalities. A fellow named Roy took a liking to me. He was an old, impeccably dressed and coiffed conductor with a typical pocket watch and long beard. He was never seen without a pipe in his hand. He fashioned himself as my grandpa and liked to give me advice. One day he put his arm around me and said "Paul m'boy, Paul m'boy. You want to stay out of trouble? Just stay away from them Jew bastards in New York". He then went off on an anti-Semitic rant that would have made any bigot proud. Standing behind him was his nephew, who was also a conductor. He was my neighbor and knew I was a member of the tribe. I thought he would pass out as he listened to me humor the old man by replying "Thanks Roy. You're the best. What would I do without you? Let me write this stuff down". I assume he must have told the old man I was circumcised by a Moyel since from that day until the day he retired, he would see me and run the other way.

My being of a different faith rarely caused a problem other than the occasional comment or symbol written on my crew room locker. That is except for one nutty day in Connecticut. My engineer and I had a short break every morning at a station that included a coffee shop. The manager was a European guy who stood 6'7" tall and weighed about 175 pounds soaking wet. He was skinny as a rail. While I was remitting my train revenue he walked over and said, "How come you never buy coffee? What are you one of those cheap Jews"? I have no idea why he said that since he didn't know I was Jewish and certainly didn't know I don't buy coffee because I don't tolerate caffeine well. Usually stuff like that doesn't affect me but for some reason I snapped which led to my first fight since Junior High School. I chased him into the parking garage and even though I was a foot shorter than him I had him down and by the throat while he squirmed to get away. I looked over my shoulder to see the station security guard hovering over us. He stood as big as the jerk only he was built like a brick shithouse. I got nervous and let the guy go and he ran like the wind while screaming that I was some kind of lunatic. I said to the guard "Weren't you supposed to do something"? He laughed and said he thought it was great seeing a midget beat up a tall guy. Weeks later I learned that the coffee shop manager had hanged himself. My initial thought was that he couldn't take having lost a fight to a Bar Mitzvah boy but I later learned he was being investigated for stealing from the till. Maybe he could have used a nice accountant to help him set things straight.

QUIET ON THE SET!

╟┼┼┼┼┼┼┼╢

ONE OF THE BIGGEST INSTIGATORS OF ARGU-
ments on the train is caused by passengers using
their cellphones to the annoyance of other riders. Somehow the riders seem to think they are in a phone booth as
opposed to on a packed train. We've had fistfights break
out over annoying cell phone users. In an effort to calm
things down the railroad started a Quiet Car program.
One car would be the quiet car where the riders would be
asked to keep their voices down and refrain from using
audible electronics. Because it is a rule and not a law the
railroad asked the commuters to self-police the policy. A
few folks on each train take it upon themselves to become
Quiet Car enforcers, screaming and yelling at people
making the slightest noise. They took it too far when

they demanded I speak to a passenger who ate egg salad several days a week because they hated the smell. I told them, "It's the Quiet Car, not the No Egg Salad Car"! The day they berated a wheelchair bound rider for talking too loud, I lost it and announced a temporary end to the program. One evening they demanded I tell a woman to stop talking. When I walked up to her I burst out laughing because her loud, nasally voice sounded just like Fran Drescher from "The Nanny" TV show. It was so funny and admittedly annoying, that I couldn't bring myself to tell her to dummy up.

My all-time favorite quiet car experience involved one of our most aggressive passenger enforcers. Apparently a woman was speaking softly into her phone and it was causing him to have a meltdown. He asked me to tell her to "shut the f… up". I came up behind her and heard her whispering into the phone "have a blessed Easter". I almost burst out laughing when I realized she was a nun. I returned to the guy and said "you know that broad who you want me to tell to shut the f… up? She's a nun. Do you still want me to tell her"? I said I'm not a Catholic so I can handle it. I then started walking down the aisle, making believe I was going to shut her up. The guy leaped out of his seat and grabbed me to keep me away from her. The knucklehead probably got beat up by nuns in Catholic school and didn't want to relive the experience. Have a blessed Easter.

GIVE EM' A HAND

ABLE-BODIED PASSENGERS WHO CAN'T FIGURE out how to use a ticket machine or travel successfully from point A to point B are annoying as hell. However, taking care of special needs passengers is something all conductors take pride in. One regular commuter had no arms but was somehow able to function well using just his feet. He would regularly "hand" his ticket to the conductor by presenting his foot. Planted between his first two toes was his monthly commutation ticket. We would have fully limbed riders hem and haw over having to show their ticket every day yet this fellow despite his challenges never complained. I have to admit though that I always assigned the newest conductor to his car just so I could see his face when the passenger's toes rose up in the air.

That passenger had a damn good reason for using his toes but nothing is more annoying than passengers that fail to exercise any common sense at all when it comes to their ticket. What could be worse than requesting a ticket only to have the rider pull it out of his dirty sneaker, sock or bra? The regular occurrence of walking up to a rider only to see his ticket in his mouth was also a little disconcerting. Happens all the time but my tolerance for it weakened as the years went on. An engineer who is a close friend of mine had transferred from conductor. One of several reasons he decided to transfer was the lack of ticket etiquette. A migrant worker once tried to hand him a bloody twenty-dollar bill for his fare. He appeared to have a gash on his hand. When the conductor refused to accept the bill the passenger proceeded to lick the blood off it and hand it back to him. Somehow a career as a locomotive engineer started to look quite appealing.

Over the years I developed an affinity for sight deprived passengers because of the respect and admiration I have for them. Only once in my career did I ever meet a blind passenger that I wanted to wack over the head. This fellow's seeing eye dog was a cute little yellow lab that looked much like my own dog. Unfortunately, he was known for verbally and physically abusing his guide dog, even lifting him in the air by his leash and choking him. I fantasized about sneaking up behind him and cutting the leash so as to free the poor little pooch from his nightmare. One day as we pulled our train into his station we saw the passengers on the platform frantically waving for us to stop. Upon stopping short of the platform we observed the blind guy had fallen off the platform and onto the tracks. The passengers said it was the weirdest thing in that it appeared that his guide dog had intentionally walked him right off the platform. It didn't seem strange to me at all. I gave that little pooch a hug and a kiss while we awaited the arrival of the ambulance.

Another of my favorite commuters is a sight deprived gentleman who despite not having a guide dog is so comfortable aboard our trains that he folds up his cane and makes his way right down the aisle. He boarded my train one evening after I had only met him once or twice. I immediately rushed up to him and offered my arm for assistance. I then led him down the aisle to an occupied seat that was designated as priority seating for the handicapped. I told the non-handicapped guy sitting there to get up but he looked at me like I was nuts (I get that a lot). I then raised my voice and demanded he relinquish his seat to the gentleman I had just brought over. He grudgingly did so and I gently assisted the other guy into the seat. It was at that point that I realized I had the wrong guy and he wasn't blind at all. I had kicked the first guy out of his seat for no reason and planted the second guy thinking he was blind. Both guys just stared at me like I was bat shit crazy. I walked away without even trying to explain it leaving the two of them to figure out the seating arrangement.

That same blind passenger liked to give me the business too. Our train became disabled on three consecutive nights. The first night our engine's computer reported low oil pressure. On the second night it drizzled and we were unable to climb a hill because we had no sand and on the third night we had sand but it was all clogged up in the automatic sanders and once again we couldn't get up the hill and had to call for buses. The next day the passenger presented me with the checklist below that he had prepared at home after the third breakdown.

Train Pre-Departure Check List
(prepared by your passengers)
Date:
Train Number:
Departure Station:
Oil in engine (circle one): *Yes   No*
Does engine have sand (circle one): *Yes   No*
If yes, can sand flow or is it clogged (circle one): *Yes   No*

Not one to leave well enough alone and as comedic revenge, I would often sneak up behind that sight deprived rider and sit down next to him. Without telling him who I was, I would lay my head down in his lap. He was always disappointed to find out it was me. My strangest experience with a broken down train caused quite a stir. We were instructed to wait for passengers who were coming over from the opposite platform because their train's engine was shot. The look on our passenger's faces was priceless as a bunch of midgets and an ugly woman who incidentally had a beard, boarded our train. I guess I should have informed our passengers that the train that had broken down belonged to Ringling Brothers, Barnum & Bailey Circus.

My worst case of mistaken identity didn't involve the handicapped and I'm lucky I didn't end up disabled after screwing this one up. Like I've told you, the majority of our passengers are wonderful. One night a rider who I vaguely knew but who had a bit of a non-descript face offered me a pack of salted peanuts. I declined, but my assistant accepted and said they were great. The next day I noticed who I thought was the same passenger board my train. Being the wise guy that I am, I gave him a wink and said that my assistant had enjoyed licking the salt off his nuts last night. I couldn't figure out why he looked a little steamed until I glanced down the aisle and saw the actual guy who gave us the nuts. I had picked out the wrong passenger! Man did I have some explaining to do on that one.

OH DEER!

━━━━━━━━━

AN UNFORTUNATE REALITY IS THAT TRAINS don't stop on a dime and we hit things all day long. Cars, trucks, fallen trees, people, dogs and deer... especially deer. One of my best engineers held the unfortunate dubious distinction of striking seven deer in one shot.

On a sunny Sunday I relieved a crew at a northern transfer point and took their train and engine to upstate New York to bring the weekenders back to Manhattan. When we pulled into the station the folks awaiting us started screaming and shielding their kid's eyes. Unbeknownst to us, the previous crew had struck a deer, which wasn't that unusual. Unfortunately they failed to tell us that the massive doe was impaled on the front knuckle of the train. It looked like a comic drawing of a dead animal with X's for eyes and its tongue hanging out. The people kept screaming at us like we were murderers even though we weren't even aware of it. It did make quite a hood ornament though. Over the years I accumulated quite a few antlers from unfortunate train hits and struck a variety of animals, including an obviously pregnant otter which for some reason bothered me more than most of the fatalities. Many engineers never get hardened to the emotion of hitting dogs on the tracks. For some reason, a cat will see the train coming and jump clear of the tracks. However, for a dog the two small running rails might as well be three feet high. Somehow the rails seem to hypnotize dogs and they refuse to jump out from the gauge of the tracks. I've been on trains that were quite delayed because a dog would run like hell but wouldn't jump off the track and the engineer refused to run him over. I recall one dog that we followed for a few miles in the Bronx much to the dismay of the railroad. I was actually kind of surprised that the majority of the commuters supported us despite the delay to our train.

One late evening I was working with an engineer who wasn't known for being particularly warm and cuddly. On our last train home he threw the train into emergency and told me he hit a deer. In light of the fact we hit deer all the time I asked why he dumped the train. He replied that it was a newborn fawn and I needed to come up to take care of it. I told him "You hit it, you take care of it". Knowing I'm an animal lover he convinced me to jump off the train and look for the fawn. The delay certainly didn't thrill my commuters who were looking to head home. The odds of a fawn surviving a train hit are near zero. However, much to my surprise I found the infant deer very much alive but with a broken rear leg. I told the engineer to throw me his coat so I could wrap the fawn and bring her aboard. When we got to the train yard I jumped in my truck and placed the fawn on the seat next to me. She wouldn't stop bleating either in pain or for her mother. I ended up calming her down by driving home with her on my lap. When I got home about midnight my family and even my dog set out to comfort the little bugger while I had a few beers and dialed up a friend who is a wildlife rehabilitator. She told me to treat the fawn like any newborn and head to the store for formula and a baby bottle. I jumped back in the truck, which wasn't the brightest move since I'd had at least a few beers. Not having had a kid in a while I had some trouble finding the baby bottles so I asked a worker who was stocking the shelves. He told me what aisle they were in but kept staring at me like I was some kind of nut. When I got to the register with the baby formula and bottles the cashier's eyes were bugging out. I couldn't help but notice that when she took my money her hands were trembling. I left Stop & Shop thinking their night workers were cuckoo. At least that was until I glanced down and realized for the first time that my shirt was covered in blood from having the deer on my lap. There I was, covered in blood in a supermarket at 2:00 a.m. looking for baby formula and bottles! I drove home scared shitless, figuring the workers had called the cops and I'd be pulled me over any second. Fortunately I made it home and the fawn made it to a vet the next morning.

This poor little guy didn't make it but did prove birds and dinosaurs are related!

ONE, TWO, TREE

━━━━━━━━━

THERE AREN'T VERY MANY MISGUIDED ELE-
phants on our tracks so hitting animals doesn't pose
the danger of hitting trucks, cars and trees. Striking fallen
trees is a fairly regular occurrence but one experience took
the cake and almost took my life. Our railroad actually
had a conductor lose her life when her train struck a fallen
tree. That tragedy weighed heavy on my mind when the
following incident happened. My engineer was an old
time freight engineer who transferred to our railroad
when the freight business slowed down between Connecticut and Massachusetts. We were working the first
passenger train south out of northwest Connecticut at
7:00 a.m. on a Sunday. I find it ridiculous, but trains
rarely reduce their speed due to poor visibility. I still laugh

when I recall the time I was berated because my engineer had delayed our train because he couldn't see what was ahead of him in blinding rain. The trainmaster actually instructed me that "the engineer doesn't need to see where he's going". He expected us to just blindly follow the signals and keep the train on time. This particular morning, we were operating in dense fog that had reduced visibility down to near zero but we were expected to maintain track speed. I was standing next to my engineer in the operating cab which had doors on both sides and a door directly in front of me at the head end of the train. Despite the fact that I was looking forward, I couldn't see a thing through the fog. All of a sudden I heard I heard the engineer yell "look out!" At the same time I felt him shove me back into the passenger coach. We struck a tree with such force that the first coach momentarily lifted off the rails, crashing down so hard that the lights went out and the A/C blowers went off which caused an eerie silence throughout the car. Just as I came to my senses, what sounded like a second explosion tore through the front door of the train. We had initially struck a tree that was lying perpendicular to and across the tracks. Rolling over that trunk was what made the front coach lift into the air. Unfortunately, there was a second tree that was pointed directly at the front of our train. That second bang was that second tree smashing in the front door. It demolished the engineer's compartment and came streaking down the aisle, scraping the ceiling. Fortunately, at that hour on a Sunday, we only had a dozen or so passengers

in the front car. I checked on them and they were traumatized but no one was seriously injured. It then dawned
on me that not only was the operating cab demolished,
but I didn't know where my engineer was. I called his
name but there was no answer. In the aisle was the torn
hemorrhoid pillow that he sat on as well as one of his
shoes. All I could think of was that I would have to be the
one to call his wife with the tragic news. After what was
probably seconds but what felt like minutes, the train
came to a stop. At that point my engineer crawled out
from under a set of seats. I didn't know whether to hug
him or kill him for not answering me. It turned out that
as an experienced freight train engineer he was taught
that if your train was derailing you hit the deck and didn't
pop up until the train or engine came to a complete stop.
I'll never forget yelling to him "Holy shit, you saved my
life by shoving me into the coach" nor will I forget his
reply, "I didn't save shit. You were blocking the exit"! My
nickname for that engineer who became a close friend
was Grandpa but even my real Grandpa never saved my
life. To say I owe him big time is an understatement.

It's ironic that our northwest Connecticut train line is
considered a "branch line" in light of the fact we hit so
many trees there. One unusual incident happened when
we hit a fallen tree while traveling through an old growth
forest with few if any houses nearby. We tried everything
to dislodge the tree from under our cowcatcher. The cowcatcher is a device on the front of a train that's meant to
deflect obstructions off the tracks thereby protecting the

electronics and air hoses located under a train. Obviously, in this case it didn't work. While we waited for the track department to show up with chainsaws, we saw a tiny old man with a gray beard hanging down to his belly button emerge from the forest. He was holding a handmade bow saw and he looked like an elf. The unusual little fellow cut up the tree with that old bow saw and we were able to get on our way, none the worse for wear. I thought I was hallucinating as he faded back into the forest barely having said a word. Not quite as strange as when an engineer operating alongside the Hudson River delayed a train while reporting that a UFO was hovering in front of him, but certainly weird nonetheless.

IS THAT A CHICKEN IN YOUR POCKET OR ARE YOU JUST HAPPY TO SEE ME?

|⊷⊷⊷⊷⊷⊷⊷⊷⊷⊷|

A T TIMES, WORKING SEVEN DAYS A WEEK HAD ME really missing my family. To keep my spirits up I started carrying a small, squeaking, particularly lovable rubber chicken. I'd carry her when working on my scheduled days off and keep her sticking out of my uniform pocket. When passengers would ask about her I'd tell them that she was Bernice the Overtime Chicken. As time went on she started making more regular appearances. My passengers seemed to look forward to the squawk at the end of my PA announcements and renamed her Bernice the Wonder Chicken. Having a rubber chicken in your pocket keeps everything in perspective and even kept some of the more demented passengers away. I guess the secret is to out-crazy the crazies. One morning I snuck up behind one of my blind, regular passengers and started squawking Bernice into his ear which made him leap out of his seat. My assistant conductor approached the passenger and said, "Don't let it bother you. Bernice always acts like an asshole when she's drinking". Bernice became a bit of a mascot and I actually received several rubber chickens as gifts from passengers. I was even given a crystal Christmas tree ornament in the shape of a rubber chicken from one particularly close rider. It once dawned on me that if I ever really did crack up it wouldn't be just a case of carrying a rubber chicken. If I ever actually went nuts I think I'd like to dress up like a secret service agent with an earpiece and dart all over the train and maybe supermarkets like something big was about to go down. Accompanied of course by Bernice.

Bernice was quite the Chick Magnet

COPPER CAPERS

T HERE ARE FEW FOLKS IN OUR SOCIETY MORE heroic than our police officers. Regardless of where they serve, the pressure and scrutiny they face on a daily basis is incomparable. Many railroads employ their own police force and ours was no exception. Over the years, I've met several railroad cops who were not only gentlemen, but consummate professionals. The duties of railroad police officers dramatically changed after the events of 9/11. My respect and admiration for them has grown in recognition of the role they serve protecting our transportation systems from those who would do us harm. For some reason however, my dealings with railroad gendarme were often less than stellar. During most of my career there always seemed to be an adversarial relationship between train cops and train crews. Fortunately that now seems to be changing for the better. Like most conductors, I avoided calling the railroad cops due to the fact that the situation was rarely resolved to my satisfaction. Another reason to avoid calling was that the railroad gave us a hard time about trains being delayed, even when the police were involved. However, the more important reason I avoided summoning them was that I often felt there was a 50/50 chance I would somehow end up getting arrested instead of the perp.

There were of course occasions where it was a good thing the police weren't summoned. In the "good old days" conductors rarely depended on the police to resolve on-board passenger disputes. If a rider was drunk, obnoxious or refused to pay, we would literally throw them off the train. Usually we waited until the train came to a stop. If we couldn't handle the situation we'd try to contact the cops and they would remove them from the train. If the passenger was abusive to the cops they would sometimes "trip" and fall down the station steps. That system despite its effectiveness, ended a few decades ago. I was astounded by an incident I witnessed many years ago while deadheading to work. A man in his twenties told the conductor in no uncertain terms that he was boarding with his bike. At the time, bicycles weren't allowed on our trains. The conductor was over seventy years old but as a former boxer he was in great shape. He politely told the passenger that he couldn't board. The young lad told the conductor to go f... himself and pushed his way past him onto the train. I was surprised to hear the conductor give the engineer the okay to proceed out of the station. As the train picked up speed I was amazed to see a bike flying out the door. Even crazier was the sight of the young guy trying to emulate Superman as he flew out the door behind the bike. Apparently he couldn't fly but he must have known how to tuck and roll since he boarded my train a few weeks later. He was very cordial after his incident and never again tried to board with his bike.

Personally, I was never a big fan of bikes on trains and I wasn't too thrilled when the railroad started issuing permits for them. There's simply no room for another tripping hazard. When the permits were issued they clearly stated that bikes were not allowed on rush hour trains. Sure enough, a young lady boarded my rush hour train with a bicycle. She looked like a greatly improved, sexier version of actress Pamela Anderson. She was wearing tiny cut-off jeans and a tight white tee shirt. For some unfathomable reason, I told her she had to get off the train. The male passengers on that train nearly kicked my butt for throwing her off. Fast-forward about twenty years and a similar looking woman boarded my train and immediately threw her shoes up on the seat. I should have been looking at her hoo-ha but instead I told her to take her shoes off the seat thereby killing my view. I guess every twenty years I make the same dumb move.

There were certainly many occasions when police intervention was warranted. The first of at least three times

I had a knife pulled on me I was working aboard a local commuter train in New York. I gave it the old "tickets please" and instead of pulling out a ticket the passenger pulled out an open Swiss army knife. He then said "You may think this is funny, but I'm going to rob you with this knife". Perhaps because the guy seemed a little meek and mentally ill I didn't feel overly threatened. The fact it was a Swiss army knife as opposed to a switchblade didn't hurt either, so I responded back "Yeah, that's f...ing hilarious". The poor guy seemed a little shot so I didn't really want to see him arrested but I called the cops anyway just in case. We waited and waited but no police showed up. Finally, the dispatcher had enough of the delay and ordered me to open the doors at which point the guy wandered off. By the time we got to our last stop I was exhausted and ready to head home. I had an old beat up station wagon in the train yard and a young pregnant wife at home. Just as I was about to head for home, I got a call that the cops caught the guy and needed me to drive down to press charges. They wanted me to drive over an hour south to a police facility adjacent to a train station on a different rail line. I told them that since it was 1:00 a.m. and I had an old jalopy and a wife due to give birth with my first child, they should just let the guy go. They managed to guilt me into pressing charges by saying they risked their lives apprehending the guy and that they would have an officer pick me up and drive me down there. After about an hour's drive I realized they were bringing me to the wrong station. When I questioned why, the cop said he was going off duty and another cop would pick me up and take me the rest of the way. I finally made it to the police facility about 2:30 in the morning. The police station was temporarily relocated into a mobile trailer because the station was under construction. At that late hour there was no one in the trailer except for the Sergeant, myself and the poor schmuck who was banging his head against the side of the trailer. The sergeant asked if I could identify him and I laughed and said, "well it ain't you or me". Me and the Sarge seemed to be getting along famously. Finally about 3:30 a.m. he thanked me and said I was free to go. I said "go where" since I worked on a different rail line, lived in a different state and the cops had driven me down there. The cops had gotten me to agree to press charges under the premise that they would drive me down there but they had no intention of bringing me back! I eventually pleaded with an officer to drive me to a station on my original rail line and made my way home about 8:00 in the morning. I don't know which was worse. Dealing with my upset, pregnant wife or watching that Sergeant rise through the ranks. I had a difficult time trusting railroad cops again after that incident.

My intention is not to blast the cops so I'll include just one more cuckoo copper incident. One of my regular riders was a young, married fellow with two small kids. He was quiet and an absolute gentleman. Every morning he'd share a smile and wish me a mellow good morning. That is, except for one fateful morning. I went to check his ticket and his eyes were bugging out of his head. I thought perhaps Dunkin Donuts screwed up and put espresso into his large coffee. When I asked him what was wrong he just pointed down at his lap where I couldn't help but notice that he appeared to have pee'd himself. I asked him why he had gotten on the train instead of heading back home to change his clothes. He replied that he was too traumatized to think straight. The poor guy was taking a wiz in the train station bathroom when two cops burst in and pointed a stun gun at him. He turned to them in a panic to say he hadn't done anything wrong. Unfortunately, when he spun he made quite a mess out of himself. The cops told him that they received a report of a possible suicidal guy in the restroom. He told them he wasn't suicidal before but he's thinking about it now! He told me that he was thinking immediately after the cops left that at what point did they see him standing at the urinal with his dick in his hand and say to themselves, "here's a guy who looks like he's about to kill himself".

Conductors come in all shapes, sizes and personalities. However, every man or woman conductor regardless of their physical or mental toughness has experienced the fear of dealing with crazed, violent passengers. I was always amazed by the incredible transformation of their temperament when the cops arrived on the scene. The funniest one I experienced involved what appeared to be a mentally unstable gentleman who was much bigger than I was. He gave me a senior citizen ticket even though he was nowhere near 65 years old. When I told him the ticket was no good and he needed to purchase a full fare he went apeshit. He started screaming almost unintelligibly that he was going to beat me to death. I realized I was in trouble and radioed for the police. I then headed to the front of the train in an effort to get away from him. Once he realized we were waiting for the police he came charging through the train, knocking people over in the aisles. My assistant was a smaller fellow but he was a deacon in his church and had excellent people skills. He jumped between us in an effort to protect me and calm down the savage beast. He kept trying to get at me and continued to rant and rave like a maniac. When the police arrived I let them know that the guy was deranged and dangerous. However, once the police confronted him he transformed into the most polite and civil person you could ever imagine. I couldn't believe it was still the same guy. It was a good thing the passengers were there to back up my story or it would have ended poorly for me. I wasn't immediately aware that when he initially threatened me there was another person in the car. He was a railroad worker who was all excited to let me know he not only had my back but also had videotaped the crazed passenger threatening me. When I viewed the video you could hear him screaming and threatening to kill me. However, the video was fixed on the ceiling of the railcar. My co-worker was hiding under the seat when he shot the video. Instead of having my back, he was scared too and videotaping what he probably thought was my demise for Youtube.

My memory bank is filled with visions of the most

violent passengers. On one late night trip I had just two of the three train cars open. A rider who looked like he had just escaped from prison told me the bathroom was dirty and he wanted to use the one in the closed car. I had my personal belongings in there including a camera so I told him he couldn't go into that car. After a heated argument he pulled a knife on me and threatened to "cut me" if I didn't let him do as he pleased. I only look stupid so I let him into the closed car but while he did his business the police were summoned. I was concerned about him being armed and time was of the essence so I bypassed the railroad police and requested a passenger dial 911. The local police force was already waiting when we pulled into the next station. I warned them in advance about the knife so they immediately wrestled him to the ground. They contacted me later to thank me because the perp had two outstanding warrants for his arrest in New York City and they would be shipping him down there when they were done with him. As they dragged him away he yelled out that he would get me and I'm a dead man. I guess he got over it since as far as I can tell I'm still here.

I had an eerily similar circumstance happen a year or two later on the exact same train. A passenger threatened me to the point that my hands were shaking. Usually when that happens I'm shaking because my blood pressure is through the roof. In this case I think I was shaking because I was scared out of my wits knowing I had no chance against this guy. I called for the police but they were nowhere to be found. Fortunately, I found a way to avoid him at the last stop and put my train away in the yard. I was still a shaken mess when I drove home from work and stopped at the local gas station, which I frequented at least once per week. I pulled into the gas station and my hands were still shaking as I filled up my truck. I drove off but after a block or two I heard screaming coming from behind me. I looked into the rearview mirror and saw the fat, slovenly gas station attendant chasing after me on foot. My mental state being what it was, I had inadvertently driven off without paying for the gas. I pulled over and the guy started cursing at me like a lunatic. I apologized and tried to tell him what I had just gone through on the train but he just kept cursing at me. I even told him that he should have known I was good for it since I'm in there all the time and always made a point of saying hello. It appeared there was nothing I could do to quiet or calm the guy down. After handing him the money, and with my hands still shaking, I offered to drive him back to the gas station. He rejected the ride, kept screaming, and told me to go to hell. I headed home and tried to calm down before I had a heart attack. By the next morning I was good as new. In a Father Knows Best moment, I strolled down to the end of the driveway to pick up the newspaper and then returned to my kitchen for breakfast. While my wife and young daughter looked on, I removed the local paper from its plastic sleeve and my eyes nearly popped out of my head. There on the front page was a photo of the gas station attendant with the headline "Gas Station Attendant Murders Girlfriend"! It was the guy who had chased after me the night before! To this day, I don't know if he was nuts and would have murdered her regardless, or if I somehow set him off and it could have easily been me he killed. I think it may be time for an electric car.

THE HAMMER

━━━━━━━━━

CONDUCTORS HAVE FACED ALL MANNER OF threats, including knives, guns, angry husbands and even on one occasion a hammer. A crazed rider wielding a full size tool attacked a conductor who for obvious reasons acquired the moniker "The Hammer". The funny thing is that this conductor's appearance was often compared to Fred Flintstone. Despite getting clocked in the head, he made a full recovery and seemed no worse for wear. We all know you can't take out Fred Flintstone with a hammer or Barney Rubble would have done it a long time ago.

Train and engine crews are a close-knit fraternity and practical jokes between co-workers are common. Despite being a great guy, the Hammer was certainly subjected to his share of pranks. Sometimes his assistant conductor would announce over the P.A. that everyone should feel free to congratulate the conductor up front (Hammer) who had just had twins, which he obviously hadn't. Every week or so the assistant would announce that it was the Hammer's birthday, resulting in his getting inundated with happy birthday wishes from the riders. The final straw was when the assistant announced that if any families were riding with young children they should make their way up front so they can meet Fred Flintstone. After that, I'm told that Hammer made it a point to come into work early each day so he could turn off all of his train's P.A. systems. One morning The Hammer informed me that he had a "Kosher headache". Knowing he had been hit in the head with a hammer, I asked what that meant and with a wink and a smile he pointed to his forehead and said "Temple to temple". The Hammer will be remembered long after his retirement for his sense of humor and unique persona.

Another buddy nicknamed Crash and I spent a while trying to out-prank each other. This went on for quite some time. I discreetly placed a brake shoe from a massive locomotive into the bottom of his workbag. He dragged it around all day while trying to figure out why he was sweating his butt off. Then Crash got a hold of my cell phone and changed the language to Japanese. It's all fun and games until you realize that neither of you speak Japanese so you can't figure out how to change it back to English. It took several trains and several announcements until I found a rider who was fluent in Japanese who could change it back to English. In light of the fact both Crash and I are fairly liberal and open-minded, I taped a large sign to the back of his Jeep reading, "Honk if you support gay rights". It wasn't until he arrived home and his wife saw the sign that he realized why all those folks were honking, waving and winking at him. Not to be outdone, Crash tucked a trail of toilet paper about eight feet long into the back of my uniform belt. Dozens of passengers laughed their asses off as I collected tickets while dragging toilet paper down the aisle. Eventually one rider took pity on me and tipped me off. I believe we called a truce after that one.

The worst prank, or best one depending on your perspective, involved two conductors who were known for being obnoxious. One morning they jumped their engineer and held him down while removing most of his clothes. They then proceeded to cover him in syrup and dumped a bag of wood shavings over him. That was actually the good news. The bad news was that a supervisor boarded at the next stop with the intention of riding the front end with the engineer. It must have taken major ingenuity to divert the boss's attention all the way into the city, thereby preventing him from seeing a semi-nude engineer looking like a monster in a cheap 1950's horror movie. Those conductors actually liked that engineer. You can only imagine what they did to guys they didn't like.

ONE BIG
(slightly dysfunctional)
FAMILY

┡┼┼┼┼┼┼┼┤

RAILROADERS THE WORLD OVER, DEVELOP A bond that is virtually unshakeable. Having experienced that emotion, I can't fathom the magnitude of the closeness of other professions such as firefighter. It's an emotional sight seeing grizzled old conductors break down in tears at retirement upon the sight of their final commuters. Locomotive engineers emotions run high as their final train pulls out of the station for the last time while detonating celebratory explosives in rapid succession under the wheels of their engine. These poignant farewells are a testament to the fact that railroading really is more than just a job.

The fraternity of our workplace is never more evident than when we suffer the tragic line of duty loss of a co-worker. Thankfully, our railroads are safer than ever. However, over the course of my career I have experienced the loss of several wonderful co-workers and friends. Each passing remains with us forever and lessons learned from their loss are passed on to future generations of railroaders in an effort to save other families from heartbreak.

Railroad supervisors usually come from the ranks and are therefore an important part of the fabric of the railroad. At one point a railroad general superintendent issued a letter to the Trainmasters, who were the conductors' bosses, and Road Foremen who were in charge of our engineers. That letter informed the supervisors that as the new general superintendent he expected his trainmasters and road foremen to treat the train and engine service workers with respect. He would no longer tolerate employees being verbally abused or demeaned by their supervisors. As the secretary of our union I received a copy of the letter and happened to fold it and place it in my uniform ticket pouch for further reference. Upon arriving in the train yard that evening I heard our train scrape against a sign that had been installed too close to the tracks. It wasn't near enough to cause any major damage but close enough to mar the paint job. I contacted the dispatcher now known as a rail traffic controller to let him know the sign was fouling the tracks. Apparently the trainmaster had plans for the evening and was not too thrilled with the prospect of driving up to our train yard.

He observed our train scrape the sign but to make me look bad he got on the radio and told the dispatcher that I was nuts and the sign was in the clear. I assume he then planned to try to move the sign out of the way. Much to his dismay, when he was finished with his transmission I keyed open the transmission button on my radio and the dispatcher heard the screeching and scraping as we continued past the sign. Needless to say the trainmaster wasn't too thrilled with my having one-upped him. He confronted my engineer and I with what was possibly the most profanity-ridden diatribe I've ever heard. When he was completely screamed out I pulled the letter from the superintendent out of my ticket pouch and asked if he received his copy or would he like me to read it to him? I think he came damn close to passing out, then ran to Dunkin Donuts and bought us a box of coffee and enough donuts to feed an army if we would forget the entire incident. Timing is everything in life.

One trainmaster made quite a name for himself from one incident. The story had it that he came upon a section of railroad that led to a bridge and where much to his surprise and shock the rail was missing. He declared an emergency on the radio thinking he was about to prevent a potential train wreck caused by the stolen rail. Unfortunately he somehow missed the bulletin order informing employees that the section of track in question was out of service for maintenance thereby explaining the missing rail. So much for contacting scrap yards looking for our purloined track.

I didn't get in trouble often over my career but when I did it was kind of silly. Due to Congress's inability to pass a budget the federal government was shut down for a few days. Wouldn't you know it that I get caught by a Federal Rail Administration inspector for failing to use the word "over" after a radio transmission? Leave it to me to get reprimanded for the first time by the Feds when the freakin' government was supposed to be closed for business.

My worst experience over the years that still affects my health also admittedly affected my attitude toward one railroad trainmaster. Our railroad decided to buy a few used engines from Amtrak. After having pulled the Amtrak Autotrain for several years, these engines' best days were way behind them. Smoke billowed from them and filled the cars to the point that the passengers and I would get nauseated. Eventually I couldn't take it anymore and reported that the smoke was making me ill. I would arrive home looking like I had pneumonia. Finally a supervisor showed up to report on the situation. As we rounded the curve our engine's smoke nearly blackened the sky. It turned out that engine was burning 55 gallons of lubricant per day when like an automobile it shouldn't have been burning any oil at all. I can still hear that supervisor reporting that he observed no smoke condition, even as the smoke billowed and filled the sky. I ended up in an emergency room where the doctor reported that I had smoke induced asthma, which is pretty strange since he had reported he saw no smoke. And they wondered why I sometimes had an attitude.

I owe a great debt of gratitude to a trainmaster who saved me from getting in serious trouble. I was senior to a fellow conductor and he wanted to drive me off a particular assignment so he could secure it for himself. My co-worker not only set me up so as to violate a major rule, but placed me in serious danger. A trainmaster who was a good, honest man, intervened and was actually demoted after telling the truth about the incident and his unintentional involvement in it. He was man enough to tell the truth, enabling me to get off the hook, but he paid a great price for his honesty.

Despite a few run-ins with management, I would be less than honest if I didn't convey the fact that several of my immediate supervisors at the time of my retirement were some of the finest I ever met. There were certainly a few notable exceptions but for the most part they were intelligent, caring folks and I came to appreciate the difficulty of their duties.

STEWIE THE STINKBUG

|◼◼◼◼◼◼◼◼◼|

UPON REPORTING FOR DUTY, CONDUCTORS MAY find they are not alone on their equipment. In inclement weather, the homeless may find a way to squeeze their way into a desolate coach. Frequently a bird can be found desperately flying around a closed car. I spent many a morning shooing them out so as not to seal their fate by carrying them into Grand Central. Over the years I've dealt with lost dogs that had made their way onto a platform and boarded with the passengers plus wayward birds, giant moths, bats, and of course there was Stewie.

As their seniority grows, conductors tend to either pick cushy assignments or the ones with the most overtime. Several years ago I picked a run that was so quiet it was almost boring. On this run all my trains stayed up in the boonies and I never travelled into the big city. One morning my engineer and I noticed that there was an unusual looking bug in the operating cab of our train. I checked it out further and came to the conclusion that it was a very cool insect called a Rhinoceros Beetle. For several days we had the same set of equipment and sure enough each morning he was still hanging out in the cab. As a joke I named him Stewie. My engineer and I developed a bit of a demented relationship with him, wishing him a good morning and even handling him a little. We arrived to work one morning only to learn that this set of equipment was going to be shipped to New York for inspection. After our first southbound train my engineer said his goodbyes to Stewie, they shook hands (okay, I made that part up), and the engineer headed to the other end so we could head north. Like usual the train was nearly empty so I settled into the rear seat and started reading the newspaper. Out of the corner of my eye I spied something. Stewie had made his way down to the floor, walked out of the operating cab, and was now trying to make his way down the aisle. At his current rate of speed I figured it would take him a week to make it down the aisle. I made an announcement telling the people to avoid Stewie in the aisle when getting off at their stop. They got into it, watching him and yelling at the few boarding passengers not to step on him. By the time we reached our last stop, Stewie had made it through about a quarter of the car. Since Stewie had never left the cab before I figured he really didn't want to go to New York and deserved to live. I emptied a small water bottle and put Stewie inside. This particular engineer was in the habit of removing a few twigs off a pine tree that was right outside his window at one of our stops. He would adorn the inside of his engine with the pine boughs. I don't know if he really liked Christmas or was just a big fan of conifers. Me and Stewie headed up to the engine and grabbed a few pine needles to dress up his bottle. I brought him home that evening and introduced Stewie the Rhinoceros Beetle to my family. Much to my wife's chagrin, Stewie overwintered right in his water bottle on our kitchen counter. Come Spring, having seen the movie Born Free, I brought Stewie back into work with me to release him. My assistant conductor took one look at him and told me to kill him because he was a Stinkbug. I insisted he was a Rhinoceros Beetle but apparently the guy knew insects much better than I did. He explained that Stinkbugs are a major crop-destroying pest. I yelled at Stewie, "How could you"! Here I saved his life and he was a pest. I ended up reading up on Stinkbugs and learned that they can decimate plants. It so happened that our train yard had a bush that produced red berries. The birds would eat the berries and plotz berry juice all over our cars. A light bulb went off in my head and I decided to release Stewie onto the crappy bush. Arriving at work a few days later, I was shocked to see that the bush was nearly gone. I thought, Stewie, you are the man (bug)! Nah. It turned out that the track department thought the bush was blocking a signal and they cut it down. Here's hoping that Stewie hopped an Amtrak train and is currently enjoying his retirement years down in Florida.

MISTER POOPY PANTS

⊬⊬⊬⊬⊬⊬⊬⊬⊬

CONDUCTORS NEVER POOH-POOH THE DISCUS-sion of poo poo. A person with what I would call a normal job could wake up with the squirts and simply call in sick. However, nothing is simple on the railroad. Eventually the railroad will assign a stand-by conductor at all of our crew bases in case someone wakes up ill. That day still hasn't arrived. A train can't leave without a conductor or engineer so if we don't make it into work the train gets annulled, making for hundreds of angry commuters. Conductors are required to provide the railroad with a minimum of four hours notice when calling in sick. Waking up nauseous or with a bad stomach doesn't constitute a legitimate excuse for the railroad. For much of my career we had no sick days at all and our regular schedule was seven days a week with no days off. On more than one occasion I've told an engineer that if we pull into a station and the doors don't open, cover me, because I'm probably having an emotional experience in the bathroom. Over the years I learned many of the intimate details of our rider's lives. One particular gentleman stood out from the rest. He didn't ride every day but his personality was downright sparkling. Unfortunately, he suffered from a brutal case of irritable bowel syndrome. As soon as he boarded he would scope out the nearest restroom and sit right next to it as he awaited his inevitable, multiple calls of nature. His need to monopolize the loo almost landed me in hot water one morning. I went to bed the evening before feeling a little off and woke up a complete mess. Some kind of virus had kicked in that I can't even describe without getting a little queasy. I had awoken at 4:15 a.m. for a 5:36 a.m. report time. That hour and a half didn't allow enough time according to the railroad to call in sick so I fought my way into work. I arrived at work pale as a ghost and boarded my train with my engineer. I walked through the train and saw that we only had one bathroom on our seven-car train instead of the usual two. The odds of a train toilet flushing were about 50/50 but this one was reasonably clean and working properly. I should have known what I was in for when I leaned over to check for toilet paper. When I did, my conductor's hat fell off my head and landed directly in the toilet. The weird part is that the hat and toilet were almost the exact same dimensions, so the odds of a direct hit were pretty slim. Seeing my hat half dunked in that blue water did nothing to help my attitude. I was sure we would never make it to Manhattan without my having to hit the loo but the bathroom was working and clean so what could possibly go wrong? Trouble arrived a few stops later when Mr. Light in the Loafers boarded the train. I panicked when I saw him because with him on board I might as well have just wrote "occupied" on the bathroom door. A little further down the line the sweats kicked in but I tried to ignore them. I couldn't keep that up for long and I eventually made a mad dash for the only bathroom on the train. I almost had a heart attack when I saw the guy was no longer in his seat. The bastard was on the train's only throne. Making a deposit in my uniform pants wasn't an option so I dove off the train at the next stop and ran into the station bathroom. Meanwhile a few hundred commuters wondered what the delay was. The rail traffic controller kept calling our train on the radio demanding the nature of our delay. I radioed him from atop the toilet that we had a medical emergency and would be on the move soon. I still wonder whether he heard all the farting and flushing noises. He kept asking if the passenger needed an ambulance but I was too shaken up and not creative enough to answer him. When with an ashen pallor I returned to the train, I announced that we were delayed due to a medical emergency, which in my mind it certainly was. We arrived in Manhattan well after our scheduled arrival time. A squadron of supervisors met me on the platform in Grand Central Terminal. They proceeded to rip me a new butthole for the delay. The railroad wanted to launch a formal investigation and possibly suspend me for delaying the train. Fortunately, some creative doctors notes got me off the hook. In retrospect, "Suspended for the Squirts" would have made a nice chapter name.

After relating that story, it's nutty but true that our train crews dubbed one of my favorite commuters Mister Poopy Pants. We would pull into our final stop, unload the passengers for their connection to New York and then have a short break. Inevitably, we would pull in to the platform and there every day to welcome us was a middle-aged man hopping up and down on one leg. Every conductor made the mistake of letting him board during their half hour break. It was only a three-car train with one lavatory. He would immediately head for the john and drop a load whose smell could fumigate roaches. Eventually, no conductor would let him board until it was actually leaving time. One day I noticed that he appeared to be particularly upset so I went out onto the platform to talk to him. He told me he had to go poopy and wanted to get on the train. I asked him why; if he had to crap his brains out he didn't just use the station bathroom. He said he could only poo on our toilet, which I thought was a little weird. I'm not sure why, but I took a liking to him and let him get on, even though I would always come to regret it. One day winter day he asked me if I would make him potato pancakes because it was Chanukah. With my usual attitude I told him to make his own stinking latkes.

He said he couldn't make them himself because where he lived he couldn't have an open flame. It was at that point that I realized he lived in a group home for adults with issues. When I explained his situation to the other conductors, most of them started treating him a lot nicer. It's ridiculous to think I cooked for a commuter but he had tears in his eyes when I made him those potato pancakes.

MEMBERS ONLY

━━━━━━━━

IS EVERY GUY ON THE RAILROAD NAMED DICK? NO, but sometimes it sure can seem that way. One would think that the majority of conductors who had been fired over the years were dismissed because of drinking, stealing or missing trains. While there's some truth to that, you would be surprised to know how many railroaders have been fired for thinking with their member. The stories have run the gamut, including one fellow who was pretty much just enjoying life during the period of free love in the late 70's. He slept with a passenger twice, which was once more than his norm. Unbeknownst to him, this commuter who was no kid, had never been deflowered. She apparently thought she had found the love of her life and didn't take too kindly of his moving on. For many weeks after, he would yell out tickets please and make his way down the aisle. Instead of her ticket this passenger would simply hand him little notes. Doesn't sound like a big deal except the notes contained death threats. She finally calmed down after about a decade.

Some conductors were a little more honorable. One conductor was quite the ladies man. He refused to marry a girl he'd been dating for decades because he couldn't guarantee he'd remain faithful while working on the rails. Immediately upon retiring after forty years of railroading and over thirty years of dating that same commuter, he threw a party and married her so she would be protected with his pension. His honesty seemed refreshing and even admirable in a weird sort of way. On the other hand, some guys set world records for infidelity. One old-timer worked a long assignment that resulted in his having an overnight layover several days per week. The rest of the crew made do by sleeping in the rail yard bunkroom. This fellow always made himself scarce for the night. It wasn't until he passed away that his co-workers found out where he was staying. At the time, the railroad provided a $2000.00 death benefit. Upon his demise, two different families laid claim for the two grand. Apparently, the old-timer had a family on each end of the rail line. His wives and kids didn't find out he was a major two-timer until his passing. Needless to say, they weren't particularly thrilled about meeting each other.

A joke was told about a man who lost his penis in an

accident only to have it replaced with a baby elephant's trunk. He claimed the thing had a mind of its own and would steal baked potatoes off the table and shove them up his butt. Just like that guy, we had no shortage of co-workers whose member thought for itself. Many moons ago a small group of conductors and engineers formed a club some referred to as "Hung Low". While it may have sounded like a Chinese restaurant it was rumored to have limited its membership to those who were incredibly endowed. The club members would whisper their secret message into the ears of select commuters, invariably leading to short term relationships. Unfortunately a supervisor eventually caught wind of the club and quickly dismembered it.

Not every conductor had the same relationship goals. One guy was particularly tough to figure out. He was about 40 years old, tall, dark and handsome. He would have had no problem getting his pick of the on-board ladies. For years though his co-workers thought he was crazy because he was shacked up with a retired commuter who was nearly 80 years old. I expressed my condolences when she finally passed on and I eventually worked up the nerve to ask him what everyone was wondering. What the heck was he doing with an old lady when he had all these young girls chasing after him? He looked at me like I was nuts and replied that he had just spent a decade with a wonderful women who bathed him, cooked for him and even found a way to get him expensive banned Cuban cigars. He said he had the world by the cojones. Months after her passing I couldn't help but notice that he was still living in her place and now driving a brand new BMW. Maybe he wasn't so crazy after all.

Pick-up lines seemed endless for those conductors who chose to shop at the on-board meat market. One conductor inadvertently walked in on a woman who forgot to lock the restroom door. She had finished her business and was just pulling up her drawers. His eyes bugged out as she said, "I'm sorry, I'm not decent and he replied, "You look pretty decent to me"! They ended up dating.

I always enjoyed replying to one common question posed by women concerned about train transfers. They would invariably ask, "Do I have to change?" You could always count on my reply being "Don't change a thing. You look marvelous". Only once did I reply to an obnoxious women's query, "Do I need to change" with the reply "Maybe, lose the eyeglasses". She didn't think it was funny either. I'm not sure how I got away with so often saying, while squeezing past a young lady in the aisle "Be careful, if we rub tushies, I have to marry you. It's part of my religion". It was evident on several occasions that the body contact was not inadvertent on their part as they brushed past.

One morning, one of my favorite commuters boarded my train and was bursting inside to share an experience with me. She'd been riding my trains for about twenty-five years and was now nearly sixty years old. She was quite the looker in her prime and was still quite attractive. She was a successful financial advisor who never passed up the opportunity to drum up new business. One morning a gentleman boarded and sat down next to her. They got along famously and he expressed interest in her investment advice. They exchanged business cards and discussed the possibility of meeting for lunch one day to discuss potential investments. Later that day, my commuter was in a corporate meeting with all the company bigwigs when her phone started vibrating. Glancing down, she noticed it was from the well-heeled gentleman so she immediately opened the text. She said her eyes almost popped out of her head when she saw he had texted her a photo of his shlong! The bosses asked why she had such an excited look on her face and she said everything was hunky-dory. She told them she was just drumming up some new business. The kooky part was that she immediately showed me the photo, which I could have lived without. I asked her why she showed it to me and she replied that she was so excited about it she was showing it to everyone. Her husband, her hair stylist, her mailman. Everyone! Undoubtedly, some women would have been disgusted or upset. My friend on the other hand was thrilled that she still had her mojo working at her age. I thought about it after and realized that when I find a shark tooth on the beach and take a photo of it on the kitchen counter you really can't tell how big it is. You need to put a dime or something next to it to get a perspective of the real size. There were no coins next to the shlong so maybe it was actually a little fella. I guess we'll never know. I think I do know however, why the technical term for people in their sixties is sexagenarian.

THE WEAKER SEX?

━━━━━━━━━━

I THINK NOT. AT LEAST NOT IN REFERENCE TO OUR women train conductors. Multiple books have been penned referencing the sexual escapades between pilots and flight attendants. There certainly have been a few on-board train affairs between train and engine crews. However, those couplings more often than not led to marriage as opposed to a quick dalliance.

It takes a strong individual, regardless of their gender, to enforce the rules and regulations aboard public transportation. Our female conductors face daily verbal abuse and harassment from riders who assume they can be intimidated. When the first women joined our railroad as conductors in the mid 1970's there was at best a 50/50 chance that they could develop the persona to survive long-term on the railroad. However, the women who made it became excellent conductors. Only the strong survived. Our earliest women engineers faced serious challenges as well. For the most part they were excellent train operators. However, there were a few crazy experiences with one or two of those woman pioneers. Poor train handling by one engineer resulted in a herniated disc in my neck and another almost jostled me right off the side of a boxcar. The most dangerous incident was the result of an engineer circumventing a safety device known as the deadman. The deadman device would cause the train to go into emergency braking if the engineer became incapacitated. One particular woman engineer took to regularly disabling the deadman. Perhaps it should have been called a deadwoman so she would have understood the importance of the device. On one trip our train was unusually crowded so I opened the head car to passengers. She considered the head car her private domain and preferred complete privacy. My opening the head car obviously annoyed her since she came charging down the aisle to berate me. Unfortunately, with the deadman disabled; the train continued hurtling through the Bronx with no one at the controls. It was lucky that the passengers didn't make the connection that she was the engineer or there would have been hell to pay. Fortunately, that engineer is no longer operating trains. Things have evolved over the years and our women engineers are now some of the finest train operators on our railroad.

Human nature being what it is, there were naturally a

few on-board romances. In fact a major newspaper did a Valentine's Day story highlighting the many conductors, including myself, who met and ultimately married a commuter. They also reported on the successful marriages between conductors and engineers.

Despite the fact that the majority of railroaders abided by the "don't plotz where you eat" rule there were a few crazy couplings. A woman conductor was nice enough to make three male conductors the guests of honor at her bachelorette party. The swimming pool scene will go down in the annals of rail history. One of the kookiest stories involved a male, married conductor who was having an affair with his attractive female assistant. He was able to maintain the relationship by convincing her that his wife was in prison with little chance for parole. The assistant eventually became suspicious of the fact that he wouldn't allow her to come to his house. Eventually her curiosity got the better of her and she traveled to his home in Connecticut. She peeked into the kitchen window and smiled as she saw her boyfriend sharing a bag of potato chips with his sons on the living room sofa. Her smiled faded when his wife walked into the kitchen, wearing an apron and looking like the quintessential homemaker. The conductor's wife threw open the kitchen window and demanded to know who she was. The woman at the window identified herself as her husband's assistant. The wife stated that it was impossible since her husband had described his female co-worker as fat and ugly and she was certainly neither. The assistant responded that the lady in the kitchen couldn't be his wife because his spouse was in prison. Things went downhill quickly and their on-board romance derailed. However, apparently love can be delayed but it can't be prevented. I recently received word that a few decades after their initial dalliance and now in their sixties, they had eloped in Atlantic City.

I WAS LOST BUT NOW
I'M FOUND

|◄┼┼┼┼┼┼┼►|

SOME PEOPLE MIGHT BE SURPRISED AT JUST HOW honest and caring conductors are when it comes to items left on our trains. I know I'm not alone in tracking down the owners of items like lost wallets and pocket-books. I've even given upset passengers my home address so they could drive over immediately to retrieve their valuables. That's not to say we don't kid around about FOT's. FOT stands for Found On Train and I'm sure somewhere there's a railroader with 3500 umbrellas in his basement but that's certainly not the norm. I've attended weddings where a co-worker claimed that every item he was wearing except his underwear was FOT but it's just a running joke. Despite the natural temptation, we are overwhelmingly honest. The items left on a train would blow the mind of non-railroaders. More than one prosthetic limb has been retrieved, as have several sets of false teeth. I'm always surprised that crutches are left behind on a regular basis. Perhaps some conductor is doubling as a faith healer. One woman from South America had her luggage returned to her, which was fortunate since her socks were stuffed with $10,000.00 in cash. There was a $100,000.00 violin found and a conductor friend of mine turned in a bag containing $60,000.00 worth of jewelry. We often had exotic dancers ride our trains to and from strip clubs. One of my favorite FOT's involved a dancer who left a bag of sex toys on my train. I got a kick out of perusing the contents of her bag but disinfected my hands after turning the bag into the Lost and Found department. One conductor will never live down his FOT story. He found a bag full of sex tapes and turned them right in to lost and found. When his co-workers found out that he had turned the porno tapes in to Lost and Found without first viewing them, they never let him forget it.

As far as I know, there has only been one dead guy turned in to lost and found. That was made easier because he was in an urn. We did have one occasion where a dead guy was left on a train and the railroad wasn't too happy about it. A train reached its final station and apparently so did one of its riders. When the conductor swept through the train at the last stop he somehow didn't notice the guy slumped over in his seat and carried him into the train yard. Yard employees later found the body and called 911. Fortunately for the crew the coroner determined that he had died prior to the time the train went into the yard. Apparently he passed away during the trip and no one noticed. Must have been the quiet car.

Our passengers and crew are frequently unnerved by unattended packages left onboard our trains. One morning several of my regular passengers asked that I check out a large pink bag left in the overhead baggage rack. Often

our conductors will call the railroad police who more often than not, summon the services of a bomb sniffing dog. Perhaps it was the disarming pink color, but for some reason I decided to check the contents on my own without calling for police

She Was Probably da Bomb

assistance. I was surprised to find the bag filled with undergarments for an overly endowed passenger. Much to my chagrin, I never located her.

REALITY CHECK

━━━━━━━━

I REALIZE THAT I'VE PAINTED A FAIRLY ROSY PIC-
ture of my profession but you knew there had to be
some pitfalls. There's no joy in being the face of the railroad when things go in the toilet and trains break down
or are late. I've had rocks thrown at me while my head
was out the window. I've been physically threatened and
assaulted as well as being verbally abused more times
than I could ever recall. Despite all that, the toughest
part of being a conductor occurs during the worst colli-
sions we face, those involving people. It's an awful experience for the engineer who is all too often traumatized
after seeing the person and hearing the impact. However, it's the conductor who is charged with climbing
down and checking on the condition of the person who

has been struck. I always dreaded the fact that the holiday season seems to bring an increase in the number of suicide attempts. Of the several times I was involved in fatalities, one incident touched me more than the others. We struck a woman on a stretch of track known for its dramatic curve. After having the third rail power cut, I crawled under the train to comfort the woman who was struck. She had lost one of her legs as well as sustaining other serious injuries. I quickly bonded with her and held her in my arms until paramedics arrived on the scene. It broke my heart when I was told that she passed away on the way to the hospital.

Surprisingly, not every instance of a person being struck by a train ends so sadly. A year or two after that heart-wrenching incident, I was traveling the opposite direction on that same stretch of railroad when the engineer threw the train into emergency. He told me we had struck a person and by the quiver in his voice I could tell he didn't think it ended well. As I climbed off the train I expected to find a body in the gauge of the tracks. Instead I spied a guy rising to his feet, dusting himself off, gathering his belongings and stumbling off the tracks. He made it to the side and actually climbed over a small fence before stumbling away. I had to radio the dispatcher to inform him that we had struck a person but that he climbed a fence and limped away. That was one of several reports I made over the years that was kooky enough to result in an increase in the number of drug tests to which I was subjected.

An even crazier experience happened to me late one night. An earlier train had become disabled and I was sent to rescue the passengers. They had already been delayed two hours and it was after 10:00 p.m. Many of the riders had to be up early for work the next morning so they understandably had a bit of an attitude. We were just a few minutes out of our initial station when the engineer brought the train to a stop. He radioed that he might be cracking up but thought he may have seen a leg lying beside the track about half a mile back. I asked him what took him so long to stop and he said he thought he was seeing things but then got nervous and thought we should check. The dispatcher ordered me to walk back a half a mile to look for the leg, which I needless to say, hoped not to find. When I told the passengers they were about to be delayed again they flipped out on me. My walk back was particularly frightening because I had to cross a railroad tie bridge over a river in the dark. Railroad tie bridges are scary for guys who don't like heights because you have to step from one tie to the next while stepping over the gaps between the ties. The river, shone by moonlight, was illuminated below. I made it over the bridge and first found a white sneaker. I then found what looked like a rubber leg with entrails hanging out. It was adorned with a tall athletic sock. There was a wall nearby and it was right around Halloween. The lack of blood made me think that the leg was rubber and it might be a Halloween prank since I couldn't find the body. I had thoughts of another random drug test if it turned out to be a hoax. Just in case it did turn out to be a prank I took a photo of it so as to prove how realistic it looked. Regardless, I had to call the police since I wasn't going to touch it to see if it was real.

The railroad and local police determined the leg was real but they couldn't locate the rest of the body. Eventually, State Police showed up with a large spotlight. As they rotated the light I heard something stirring in the high weeds. Just as the cop and I turned to face the sound, a guy sat straight up out of the weeds. He was holding out his leg's stump and appeared to be in shock. Both the cop and I jumped out of our skin. By the time I got back to the train I was so pale I must have looked like I was in shock too because instead of berating me the passengers were genuinely concerned for my welfare. Allegedly the guy was intoxicated and laying with his leg over the rail. He was dressed all in black so all the engineer noticed was his white sneaker, which led him to believe it was only a leg. It seemed the metal wheel and steel rail cauterized the wound. There was very little bleeding which probably saved the guys life. Almost one year to the day I was informed by the dispatcher to wait for a wheel chair passenger coming over from the opposite platform. It was the same guy, drunk as a skunk. He refused to pay me saying "you guys took my leg, you ain't taking my ticket". He had no idea it was really the same crew that was on the train that struck him. He was so drunk and abusive that I told him he didn't have a leg to stand on. When he continued to carry on I let him know that his left sneaker was in my trunk if he wanted it back.

EVERYDAY HEROES

▶◀▶◀▶◀▶◀▶◀

R AILROAD GUYS HAVE ALWAYS HAD GREAT NICK-
names. Over the years I've worked with the Dancer,
the Boxer, Sudsy, Tin Can, Crash, Shady, Lump-Lump,
Johnny Shoes, Horsecock Taylor, UFO Moe, Peepshow
Bernie, Depth Charge, Footer, Coco the Chimp, Cup-
cakes, Bubbles, Flash and more recently, Bad Andy.

Most of the rail nicknames made sense. The Dancer
was light on his feet and a ladies man, the Boxer, a Golden
Gloves champ, Horsecock Taylor's ancestors probably
handled sewing and alterations. I'm guessing you can figure out for yourself how Peepshow Bernie got his nickname. Peepshow was a colorful character that never
ceased to amaze me. We were working together and
boarded opposite ends of the same train. We checked the

radio and buzzer communication system and both were working properly. When I checked the P.A. I thought I would mess him. When he answered, I asked him what track he was on. When he replied track 32 I yelled out on the P.A. that I was on track 34 and he needed to get over there right away. He actually climbed down and then up onto the other train even though we had been talking on the same internal train P.A. I think one too many peep-shows may have affected him.

Coco the Chimp was a bit of a nervous chap who made it a point to avoid conductor assignments. He pre-ferred working as an assistant conductor which held less responsibility and which greatly reduced the odds of get-ting into trouble. Even in the reduced role of assistant, he was very competent and dependable. In fact he was so dependable he would arrive at work nearly an hour earlier than his report time. This made no sense to me in that we are paid by the hour. I tried multiple times to explain to Coco that he was giving the railroad a free hour of his time every day but he insisted there was a logical reason. He stated that unlike myself, if he were to get a flat tire on the way into work he would have time to repair it. This would keep him from missing his train and losing a day's pay. I did the math for him and explained that he would be better off missing one day's pay in thirty years as opposed to giving the railroad five hours a week, equal-ing two hundred and sixty hours a year! Regardless of my calculations Coco kept coming in early. Coco the Chimp kept this up for nearly twenty years until the morning I received a frantic phone call from him. He was panicking as he told me that he was on the side of the highway with a flat tire. I laughed and told him to calm down since this was the reason he was always running early and he had more than enough time to change the tire. I laughed so hard that I nearly cried when he told me that he couldn't since he had no idea how to change a flat. The knuckle-head had come in to work early for twenty years in case he blew a tire but never bothered to learn how to change a flat. Yup, he missed the train.

Unlike the others, Bad Andy was given his name because he was the polar opposite of bad. He was just a good kid who was thrilled to be a conductor. He was also something of a train buff. Most professional railroaders want nothing to do with rail fans, who've been given derogatory terms like Foamers (foam at the mouth at the site of a train) or FRN's (f'n rail nuts). Bad Andy may have been a bit of a buff but he was universally liked and his knowledge of trains led to heroism on his part.

Most of our train crews, including me, never noticed that day after day, our trains were crossing over a huge causeway. We just assumed it was a high spot that happened to have a lake on one side. Andy though, knew his territory. One night, he was heading north on the last passenger train of the evening. As his train passed over the causeway he had a feeling something just didn't feel right. Any other conductor would have just blown it off, assuming it was just a minor flaw in the track bed. Even though it was mostly just intuitive and not a major issue going over the causeway, Andy called the Rail Traffic Controller to report it. He told him that it might be nothing but he just felt something wasn't right. Unbeknownst to Bad Andy, the entire causeway collapsed in the dark after his train passed over it. The Rail Traffic Controller was experienced and sharp. He helped avoid a catastrophe by ordering a track car, which is a pickup truck with train wheels, take a ride up the track to check it out. The track car headed north about 2:00 a.m., just a few hours prior to when the first southbound passenger train would traverse the causeway. Despite the fact it was dark and in a desolate area, the track car employees realized that the track ahead was still in place but now hanging twisted and suspended over a large canyon.

Had Bad Andy not made that call, untold lives could have been lost as the first train of the morning plunged

The Danbury Washout! Here Today, Gone Tomorrow.

into the ravine. Bad Andy's real name is Andrew Mc-Clellan and I publish it in recognition of the lives he saved that day. I don't know whether the railroad ever recognized his actions but his fellow crewmembers and commuters sure appreciate him.

Several of our conductors performed heroic actions over the years. I myself once retrieved and personally returned lost luggage to a distraught passenger. Yea, she was Miss Florida but her looks and pageant win (cough, cough) had nothing to do with it.

Just as in Bad Andy's case, the following episode didn't result in an "Atta Boy" or a handshake but if fish could talk, they'd call it heroic. Early one morning while heading south, we came around a bend and struck a fallen tree. We had a workhorse of an engine known as an FL9. The FL9 had a sight glass on the fuel tank that was basically a glass tube that allowed you to determine the fuel level. The tree smashed the sight glass and fuel started pouring out of the engine towards a river loaded with trout, beavers, otters and more. My engineer immediately tried to close the emergency fuel shut off valve only to find that the handle was sheared off in the accident. I used my hands to shovel track ballast stones in an attempt to divert the diesel fuel away from the river. At the same time, my engineer went house to house, waking up folks and asking for tools to stop the flow of fuel. He managed to amass enough tools to get the job done. I tried to nominate my engineer for recognition from the railroad but they said his actions didn't warrant it. However, a supervisor sent flowers to all the neighboring houses. My engineer may never have received a thank you after saving a fortune in environmental cleanup costs but I'm sure the fish would nominate him for "Man of the Year".

CRASH

WHILE BAD ANDY'S NICKNAME WAS BASED ON irony, Crash's name fit like a glove. Crash became one of my closest friends on the railroad despite the fact he never seemed to work much due to on and off the job accidents. As one of the more colorful characters on the railroad, most co-workers and commuters found him friendly and entertaining. However, having been born and raised in a working class section of Manhattan, he was also known for never backing down from a fight. Like most people involved in public service, Crash dealt with abusive, disruptive and arrogant customers on a regular basis. Crash was usually able to defuse most situations through the use of humor. However there were occasions when his fighting instinct would kick in. One passenger boarded his train and paid his fare but he was short $1.00. Under most circumstances being short a buck is no big deal. In this case though the passenger was raising a ruckus for no reason. Crash calmly put his hand out so as to tell the passenger he needed to calm down and lower his voice. Unfortunately the guy made the mistake of slapping Crash's hand out of the way. My buddy's testosterone level went into overdrive and a scuffle broke out. Fortunately, our regular passengers were able to get between them before a major fight ensued. Like most of us, Crash was usually hesitant to call the cops but in this case he felt it was prudent to do so. When the police arrived they were still jawing at each other. They pulled the passenger away and spoke to him for just a few seconds. They then went over to Crash and said if he wanted to press charges he could, but was he aware of the fact that the passenger was handicapped? Crash's initial reaction was that the passenger seemed physically fit but the officer meant mentally handicapped. My boy Crash had inadvertently called the cops because a mentally challenged young fellow was short a dollar. Crash couldn't believe that he hadn't noticed that the guy's cake wasn't fully baked so he went over to talk to him. Once his anger had cleared he immediately recognized that the fellow was to say the least, a little simple. It was tough for Crash to live down calling the cops on a guy who had a helmet with his name on it. To Crash's credit, he not only ended up befriending his daffy nemesis but they also became Facebook friends.

When no one was slapping his hand, Crash was actually very cordial on the train. He never shied away from striking up a conversation with a passenger. Crash was happily married but a faithful degenerate like myself. This would often lead to schmoozing with some good-looking women. For a while Crash and I worked a train together on which he would strike up a conversation with a particularly well-endowed woman. Actually, you couldn't sink her in a pool with a bazooka. If I tried to start up a conversation with her, Crash would kiddingly hip-check me out of the picture. One uncomfortable aspect of being a conductor is that a senior employee could bump you off your run. This would change your work hours and often turn your life upside down. Unfortunately for Crash, he wasn't getting along with a fellow conductor. Believe it or not, that guy bumped Crash off our train just to break his chops even though he had to take a pay cut to do so. With Crash out of the picture, and since I was never one to pass up a golden opportunity, I walked right up to that full-figured passenger. We schmoozed a little bit and then I asked her why she was all covered up with a scarf on such a warm day. She replied that she was in engineering and occasionally had to go out to construction sites. She continued that the outfit she was wearing would have caused a riot because of the "girls". I innocently told her I had no idea what she was talking about. She then gazed around to make sure no one was looking, pulled off the scarf and pulled down a few more items so as to completely expose "the girls". I quickly found out who the girls were, that they were twins, and quite spectacular. That passenger is now a good friend of both Crash and I. I guarantee he'll never forgive the guy who bumped him and made him miss out on the show. On that same trip I heard my assistant who had bumped him yell out in pain. One of our regular commuters had kicked him in the shins and said, "That's for bumping Crash". Now you know why we feel like they aren't just our commuters but our friends too.

P.S. Crash didn't get his nickname from the several minor accidents but because of one BIG one. My buddy actually came within a few feet of accidently blowing up the most famous train terminal in the world. Maybe we'll share the details of what could have been the end of Grand Central Terminal in this book's potential sequel, "I'm Still a Rear End".

I may never have come close to accidently blowing up Grand Central Terminal but I did have a few close calls over the years. The following things may or may not have happened depending on the statute of limitations. The closest I've come to buying the farm was when I lost my grip while riding the side of a work train. We were dropping ballast stone along the side of the tracks and my hand slipped off one the handrails. As the train went through a switching crossover I hung on by one hand as my rear end swung out. I came so close to a metal switch stand that my pocket caught on the edge of the stand and ripped the entire rear end out of my jeans. Another inch and ventilated jeans would have been the least of my problems. I spent the rest of the day switching out freight cars with my butt cheeks blowing in the wind.

In single track, manual block territory, there were no signals and you needed written permission, referred to as a form M, train order or simply "the paperwork" to occupy a track. A story is told (which may or may not have involved me) of a hung over conductor reaching his final destination on his northbound train, opening the phone box and signing the required forms. He then headed south with his next train. Upon arriving at a station several miles down the track, a police officer came out of the station and said the dispatcher was screaming over the public intercom. The engineer said there was no logical reason why they would be calling. He hadn't requested a copy of the paperwork or even asked to see it but he had seen his conductor open the phone box and sign the register sheet. He had faith in his conductor and just assumed he had called for permission to occupy the track and had ensured there were no trains heading towards them on the same track. Yikes! Somehow that usually competent conductor had forgotten to call for permission to occupy the track. The train crew covered their tracks by calling the dispatcher and saying that they had just arrived with the northbound and needed paperwork to head south. Meanwhile the train was already miles down the track heading south and almost at their last stop. To cover their butts, once they got the okay to head south they had to do so at five miles per hour to kill time. They misinformed their passengers that they had to travel at a snail's pace due to track problems. The train and its exasperated passengers finally arrived at their final destination and the crew never again left their initial station without written permission.

Single track, manual block territory made for many interesting experiences. Fortunately, most of the crews were experienced and there were very few fender benders. One of my trains was scheduled to have a "meet". A meet is defined as two trains heading towards each other at the same location, at the same time, on the same track. This was obviously only scheduled where there was a rail siding so one train could get out of the way, thereby avoiding a head-on collision. One train's paperwork would order that crew to "hold the main". The other train would be ordered to "take the siding". The orders regarding a meet are given by Rail Traffic Controllers (RTC's), who in addition to many other safety related duties, are responsible for routing our trains so as to avoid collision while maintaining on-time performance. Rail Traffics Controllers work behind the scenes and are therefore unknown and underappreciated by most of the riding public. They have what is most likely the most stressful job on the railroad. My RTC one day was very competent but known for his arrogance. Even though he thought he was infallible, he had made the incredible error of issuing paperwork to both trains ordering them both to hold the main. Both engineers were experienced and there was no collision but you can only imagine the look on those engineer's faces when they realized they were approaching each other headlight to headlight on the same track. I held onto that defective paperwork with the intent of throwing it in the cocky rail traffic controller's face the next time he gave me a hard time. Fortunately, he mellowed out over the years and became a nice fellow so I never felt the need to do that.

An excellent, experienced engineer was given the nickname Bubbles. He was not a morning person and often arrived at work a grumpy mess. Bubbly he wasn't, so the name stuck. He was a giant of a man. The kind of guy that would leave the owners of all you can eat restaurants shaking in their boots. He was also a very thorough engineer who would always insist on a copy of the paperwork granting us permission to occupy a section of track. One morning he was more groggy than usual and he forgot to request a copy from me. He realized it a few stations down the road and asked me to give him his copy. I thought I'd play with him a little so I refused to hand it over. He asked me whether I had made the phone call to the dispatcher and I told him it was none of his business. By the time we arrived at our last stop I thought he was going to have a nervous breakdown. The sight of an engineer twice the size of his conductor chasing him all over the train yard threatening to kill him left the yard crews in stitches. I was laughing so hard that running was difficult. Plus I didn't want Bubbles to have a heart attack so I just fell down laughing. He jumped on top of me but eventually started laughing too. Bubbles is a good man for not killing me.

A near heart stopping experience involved that same type of paperwork. In addition to giving you permission to occupy a track, it also conferred other emergency instructions. However, once you were given paperwork, the dispatcher wasn't allowed to add anything to it. If another situation arose he would have to issue new forms, which they never liked to do. It would never happen now, but at that time railroaders were sometimes lazy and instead of issuing the new form they would just give you the additional instructions verbally. This was against the rules. As you read on, the reason will be obvious. The verbal instructions that were given, and should have been written down, were to stop and protect a specific railroad crossing where the crossing gates, lights and bells were malfunctioning. Since the instructions were never issued as paperwork, he had no written directive to give the engineer and he forgot to mention it to him. As they neared the crossing in a blizzard at 50 miles per hour it caught his attention that the gates weren't coming down and the lights weren't flashing. His heart sank as he realized he had forgotten to tell him to stop. He looked to the right and saw a car sliding sideways down the hill in the direct path of the train. All he could think of was the possibility of getting charged with involuntary manslaughter. He told the engineer to notch out the engine and held his breath as they accelerated to the point that the car barely cleared the rear of the engine. He should have bought stock in Fruit of the Loom since it was time once again for new underwear.

One of the most frightening experiences I encountered was when my engine caught fire in a tunnel that extended for several miles under Park Avenue. In the event of a train fire an engineer was by rule supposed to keep his northbound train moving until it was out of the tunnel. Instead, my inexperienced engineer stopped the train to determine the intensity of the fire. Cursing on the radio is a major violation but I cursed up a storm as I screamed for him to move the train. Unfortunately once he stopped, the engine shut down and we were dead in the water. I was able to knock down the fire before anyone was hurt or killed but it took many years for me to forgive him for that blunder. On a lighter note, whenever our engine would break down I would make the announcement, "The bad news is our engine has died. The good news is we aren't in an airplane".

A railroad bartender had a much more death-defying experience. He was riding home from work, late at night in a deadhead car that was closed off to the regular passengers. His station was approaching and when the train came to a stop he used his key to open up the single door so as to step out onto the platform. Unfortunately, he was unaware the train had stopped for a red signal on the bridge just before the station. When he stepped off the train, instead of a platform he stepped out into a black abyss and fell a few hundred feet into Long Island Sound. He had no idea the train was on a bridge over water. As he fell in the darkness he was expecting imminent death from striking concrete or some other structure. He said he would have been thrilled to have landed in water except he was totally confused as to where he was. He didn't know whether he had perished and was entering a new realm or whether he had actually landed in water in which case he had no idea which way was up. Somehow he fought his way to the surface and survived his injuries. Unfortunately he never returned to work on the railroad and probably never rode a train again.

A fellow conductor experienced a near-death experience in one of our train yards. He was one of the most muscular guys on the railroad and his strength saved his life that day. Somehow he found himself between two boxcars that were being coupled together. Railroad stories were told of conductors and brakemen who were coupled between cars only to have their families summoned to say their goodbyes. The powers that be knew that once the train knuckles were uncoupled the poor soul would bleed to death. The coupler knuckles can be pushed left and right to accommodate trains that are on curves. However since they weigh upwards of 100 lbs. it is difficult to move them, even under optimal conditions. Somehow, as the train couplers closed in on my co-worker, he realized it was too late to run or dive out of the way so he placed one arm in front of him and one behind. With brute force he was able to push the two couplers out of each other's way to prevent them from lining up and crushing him. I don't know of anyone else strong enough to have accomplished that. His back was badly injured but his strength certainly saved his life.

HOW I MET YOUR MOTHER

*Authors note: This chapter may be inappropriate
for children (especially my own).*

━━━━━━━━

Wʜᴀᴛ'ѕ ᴛʜᴇ ʙᴇѕᴛ ᴛʜɪɴɢ ᴛʜᴀᴛ ᴄᴏᴜʟᴅ ᴇᴠᴇʀ happen to a single train conductor? How about dating a smoking hot, 34 year old commuter. Not only was she a 10, but she was also being treated by a shrink for nymphomania. One day she said she had a surprise for the conductor. She told him that she wanted to give her very attractive single neighbor who was a fellow commuter a special birthday present. That gift was the 21-year-old conductor! It was evident that the neighbor had never done anything like this before. However, after a bottle or three of wine, the little nymph managed to turn that birthday gift into one of the hottest threesomes you could ever imagine. It was undoubtedly, one of the greatest days in the life of that conductor. Oh sure, a threesome with two hot chicks sounds like a frolicking escapade between a few commuters and one lucky conductor. However, things are never as simple as they appear.

As the gorgeous blonde commuter allowed her dress to fall to the floor and excitement glowed in the eyes of the cute as a button brunette, the conductor throbbed with excitement. Okay, that's it for titillation. It really was bong, boing, bong. The initial bong helped create the mood since this threesome predated random drug testing on our railroads. If you are unable to figure out the boing, you probably shouldn't be reading this paragraph. The final bong was the doorbell, which was unfortunately rung by two town police officers. But I digress. Most people wouldn't think of railroading as seasonal work. However, I was laid off for much of my first few years on the job. For much of that time I worked at a local animal shelter. The bad news is that the job paid minimum wage. The good news is that shoveling dog poop made me appreciate my railroad gig and it paid the rent. As a single, unattached fellow, I lived in one of four, two room attached bungalows. The affluent, elderly landlady lived in a large home on the property and she charged a ridiculously low rent in exchange for my maintaining the property. For many years she rented all four units to single railroaders who despite being wild and crazy, caused her no headaches or aggravation. When one tiny unit became available, she compassionately rented it out to an undocumented alien and his family. Joining me in my tiny two-room shack were two dogs, a rabbit, a guinea pig, three cockatiels and two parrots. In the adjoining 300 square foot shack were the husband, his wife, two daughters and a dog that also lacked documentation. Not surprisingly, my next-door neighbors and I had clashing lifestyles. One of the parrots was an African Grey that had learned just two phrases but he had them down cold. They were "Hello Birdie" and "F... You". For some reason, the guy next-door took offense to hearing that all day long and placed a complaint with the landlady. She called and asked me to get rid of the birds. Instead, I told her that I would like to introduce her to the birds so she could see that they were sweet as a button and never uttered a curse word. If after meeting them she wanted them out, so be it. While she made her way up the hill, I rushed the two large parrots out to my van and threw blankets over their cages so as to quiet them. I then let the three little cockatiels out of their cage to greet the landlady. They immediately flew to her and showered her with kisses as I fibbed and claimed they were the only birds in the place. I shared a little schnapps with her and then she went next-door and ripped into the neighbor for complaining about these tiny, quiet, sweet little creatures. After she returned to her house I went out to the van and brought the two obnoxious birds back into my home. Naturally, as I walked past the neighbor who was still steaming on his porch, the African Grey lit up with "F… You", F… You", F… You". I still can't believe that didn't result in my demise.

While it was excellent that all five birds survived the neighbor's complaint, that incident may have precipitated the house call from the town cops that broke up the threesome. Remember the threesome? That's what this chapter was supposed to be about and where the last bong comes into play. Just as things were reaching a proverbial climax with candidate number two, the police officers entered the room. The two nudists looked up through the cloud of smoke and asked, "Shouldn't you have knocked first"? The cops made no secret of the fact they were enjoying the view of the cute brunette and laughed as they said that the front door was wide open and the dog invited them in. They explained that they had received a noise complaint and were just checking it out. Fortunately, uniformed workers, be they cops, firefighters or conductors, have a bond and the cops ignored the wonderfully aromatic smoke. Unfortunately, the tryst came to a quick end since the brunette was flipping out over the cops' entrance and the blonde was nowhere to be found. A few weeks later, I received a call from the landlady asking me to do a minor repair to the roof. While working on the shingles, I noticed one of my pasta pots lying on the roof, smashed to smithereens. I began putting two and two together and called the blonde to ask if she knew anything about it. It turned out that it wasn't the throes of passion that resulted in the noise complaint. Apparently the hot blonde, despite having set the entire thing in motion, got jealous and tried to break things up by smashing the pot against the side of the house causing the neighbor to call in the complaint.

What could have been a heartbreaking end to the story is that the gorgeous blond was dating a rich, married commuter at the same time as her conductor and was unknowingly playing me so that the rich guy would have to poop or get off the pot regarding their relationship. He finally left his family for her and she was never heard from again. There are however times in life when you realize everything happens for a reason. I needed a date for a wedding that was just days away and Blondie had left me in a lurch. Fortunately, the railroad provided for a deep dating pool. I decided to take a different tack and searched my morning train for a respectable date as opposed to some of the lunatics I had been seeing. It took no more than a few minutes to locate a sweet, innocent prospect. What was intended to be a one-time wedding date led to a wonderful four-year courtship. Who knew I'd be so enamored with a respectable young lady? It must have been quite a surprise for my family. That commuter turned out to be the absolute best thing that ever happened to me and at last count we're happily married over thirty years.

On another occasion a faithfully married conductor had the surprise of his life while collecting tickets. A beautiful young lady boarded his train and sat by herself at the rear of the last open coach. When he requested her ticket she told him that she left her wallet home and had no ticket or cash. She seemed honest and legit so the conductor told her "Don't worry. I'll be right back and we'll work something out". By work something out he meant he'd get her identification and send her a bill for the fare. She apparently misinterpreted his innocent comment to mean something entirely different. He returned a few minutes later to get her name and number for the bill and his eyes almost popped out of his head. The young lady was even more beautiful than he imagined and nothing was left to the imagination. She had removed all of her clothes and nervously said to him "I'm ready. So how do we do this"? She actually thought she needed to put out. He politely asked her to slowly put her clothes back on, emphasizing the word.... SLOWLY. He passed on the sex and probably just about passed out over the thought of what had just transpired.

NOT QUITE THE MILE HIGH CLUB

ONE EVENING I WAS WORKING A LATE NIGHT train to upstate New York. After collecting the fares, my assistant and I went into the deadhead car (closed to the passengers) to do some paperwork. Under most circumstances when a passenger unbolts a closed car and enters without permission the conductor gets pretty irritated. In this case though, it was two women in micro mini-skirts. They were very "friendly" and told us they were vacationing from Switzerland. They said they had been in New York for a week, hadn't hooked up with any guys, and would be back on the train the next night to bang us. I must have sounded like Ralph Kramden again at that point... Hamana, Hamana, Hamana. When I got home that night, my wonderful wife was looking great and my little daughter, despite having a cold, waited up to see Daddy. Major guilt trip. Even though I almost had a nervous breakdown, I arranged to switch trains the next night with an unmarried conductor who now considers me his hero.

Lest you think this only happens to young guys, I eventually reached my fifties and was a little depressed about an upcoming operation. One of the regular commuters was a big fan of mind-altering substances, yet she immediately noticed I was down. When I told her what was weighing on my mind, she sat down across from me and said, "I know what you need. You need to fuck". I said, "Fuck who?" and she said "Fuck me" and started taking off her blouse. I replied that I couldn't screw her because, A. I'm married, B. I love my wife, C. She lived in my town and D. All the passengers were watching! The regular riders were enjoying the show but I panicked and told her to put her shirt back on. She kept carrying on that screwing would relieve my anxiety and it didn't matter that I was married. I jumped up to open the doors at the next stop as well as to escape her clutches. Standing in the vestibule was a regular commuter who was an off the boat Italian guy in his 70's. Like half the car, he had heard and seen the entire thing. I nervously said to him "What am I gonna do with this?" and he replied with a thick Italian accent "Whadaya mean what are ya gonna do with it? You're gonna fuck it. You're gonna fuck it". Naturally, I didn't do it but I did tell her that I was very curious about her tattoo. I had gotten a glimpse of it when she opened her blouse. It appeared to snake its way around her breasts and disappear down toward her cha-cha. Once again she started taking her clothes off and I stopped her. I half-kiddingly told her to just send me a photo. However I did cave in a moment of weakness when she asked for my cell phone number so she could send me a few photos. Just one day later, there I was in a hospital checking out her photos with my surgeon. She was right. Even though they were just photos, she did alleviate my anxiety.

Conductors and engineers who are scheduled to work long hours are required to have rest breaks. Usually those breaks are in the main terminal or occasionally in their home crew base. Once in a while though, train turn-around time would require that rest be in less than desirable locations. At one time, my run had a two-hour break in a lousy neighborhood. My engineer and I would hunker right down in the train as opposed to going for a stroll and risk getting mugged. I was a close friend of the engineer but he made it clear to me that he considered the break "me time" and he didn't want to be bothered. He would go into a separate car and turn down the lights. He even pulled out the seat cushions so as to form a bed and collected newspapers to cover himself up and stay warm. I would hang out in the other car and read the paper or try to nap. One evening while reading the paper, I heard a knock on the side of the train. I opened the door but saw no one and resumed my reading. Again I heard knocking and reopened the door only to hear a voice down under the platform. I peered down and saw an uncomfortably skinny, disheveled young girl looking up at me. I helped her up on the train and asked her what she was doing down there and she replied that she was homeless and felt safe there. As I was about to tell her to get off the train she grabbed my hand and asked, "Do you fool around"? I told her "Sure. I have a great sense of humor". She replied "No. I mean blow jobs". I kiddingly replied "No. I don't give no blow jobs" and she went on to innocently explain that she meant getting one not giving one. She stated that she was hungry and would service me for $5.00 so she could get something to eat. I let her know that I was happily married and that would be out of the question. She then asked me if there was anyone else I could think of who would let her blow him so she could make a few bucks. Ding! The bell went off in my head as I thought about my 60-year-old buddy in the next car with a virtual do not disturb sign hanging over him. I knew the last thing he wanted was the company or the services of a young lady. I told her to go into the next car where she would see a tent of newspapers. I told her to just knock on the papers and let him know she was about to blow him. Within seconds the newspapers went flying and his glass milk bottle crashed to the floor. He was dying to kick my butt but I thanked her for helping me break his chops. For quite a while I referred to that town as the "Home of the $5.00 blow job". That was until the engineer told me she had actually offered her services to him for $3.00. He was a lot older than me and would have required a lot more time and energy but it was nice to know she offered a senior citizen discount. I'm sure it's not enough for a ticket into heaven but I did give her $10.00 for a sandwich.

There have been a ton of instances where exhibitionists or just plain old drunk or horny passengers made an on-board go of it, sometimes in plain view of the engineer or conductor. One particularly funny episode had a pair of amorous passengers going at it in the rest room. Apparently he was quite the performer because even though they were locked in the bathroom, you could hear her moaning throughout the coach. When they finished up, she emerged first... to cheers and a standing ovation from many of the passengers!

One Saturday morning I had a couple board my train and I couldn't help noticing that even though the woman had a few miles on her, she had an incredible body and wore a teeny, tiny sun dress. Within minutes of boarding, she was on top of her friend, riding him like a bronco. I went over and called a timeout, telling them that I was all in favor of their activity but they needed to move to the last group of seats in the rear of the car so nobody would see them (except me). The only problem was that I forgot that a few stations down the road, those rear doors would be on the platform and open up. Sure enough, they opened and a nice young family boarded only to see her riding this guy like it was her last rodeo. I had a tough time explaining that complaint letter.

YOU WANNA SCREW
FOR THAT?

〉〉〉〉〉〉〉〉〉〈

CONDUCTORS AND ENGINEERS ON OUR RAILROAD
work split shifts of up to 16 hours a day, 5 days a
week. To comply with federal rest requirements, the railroad provides tiny bunkrooms for conductors working
these long assignments. Because of the value of retail
space in Grand Central, the railroad located our bunks in
the catacombs of the terminal. No natural light, water
leaks, rodents, roaches and constant screeching from the
nearby subway trains. After having a large rat fall through
his bunkroom's ceiling tile, one conductor took matters
into his own hands. The conductor hand-delivered the
rat to the Grand Central Stationmaster's office causing

quite a scene. He wasn't fired but to say the railroad wasn't too pleased with him would be an understatement.

Several years ago, the TV show 60 Minutes did an expose about our train terminal. One of their famous reporters got wind of the abysmal conditions in our crew room and stopped in to interview us. He asked if anyone had any crazy stories to share and one of our zanier conductors spoke right up. The conductor said he had a great story but that 60 Minutes probably couldn't air it. The reporter asked him to tell the story anyway and they would see if they could figure out a way to air it. They aired everything except that one story mentioning that there was just no way to clean it up. That story can now be told. It involved a male passenger who enjoyed regularly relieving his stress on the back of the heads of unsuspecting riders. The shocking thing isn't that it occurred but rather the fact that it has happened many times, and not by the same guy. Maybe it's just me, but I've been about as horny on a train as you could ever imagine and not once did it ever occur to me to spank the monkey on someone's head without their express permission. Regardless, there have been more wee-wees exposed on my trains than you could shake a stick at. There's nothing like rail travel. One of the few places where you can come and go at the same time.

Eventually our union got some politicians to pressure the railroad into relocating our bunkrooms out of the dungeons and into a much better area. It was quite a sight seeing all those grown men making a pilgrimage from the old facility to the new one carrying their belongings and blankies.

For many years I was able to avoid long bunkroom jobs. I hated being away from my family for up to 18 hours a day. Despite my efforts, eventually circumstances led me onto one of those long assignments. My first few days I slept with one eye open, not only because of the conditions but also because I was afraid I'd oversleep and miss my train. When I first started on the railroad, I worked a train to Kansas City that arrived so late that we only had an hour or two before we turned back for New York. Amtrak offered me a hotel room but I was so shot and time was so short that I should have refused it. Instead I hit the sack, overslept and missed my train back. I was scared the railroad would fire me and I'd have no way back to New York. It worked out okay, but I've been a little paranoid about alarm clocks ever since.

The only illumination in my bunkroom was the tiny little red light from the smoke detector. Much to my shock, I happened to open one eye and the light was gone. I opened the other one and I could see it. Left eye, there was the light, right eye, gone. Left eye, light, right eye, darkness. This went on a few times until I was convinced I had gone blind in one eye. I flipped the light switch on in total panic, only to realize that my big schnoz was blocking the light and my vision was fine. What a knucklehead. Regardless, I knew I would never get any sleep until I bought at least one alarm clock.

My eldest daughter spent one year studying abroad in

England. At the same time an English guy was studying a broad, but my daughter was the broad he was studying. They ended up marrying and living across the pond. While they were courting, he bought her a European watch as a gift. Over time a tiny screw in the watch worked its way loose and we couldn't find a replacement screw anywhere in Connecticut. Since sleeping in the bunkroom was out of the question, I had plenty of free time and decided to head to an expensive watch repair place to see if they had the rare screw. The good news was the young, handsome fella said he had the screw. The bad news was that they wanted about 20 bucks for it even though it was the size of a small seed. While I hemmed and hawed over the price, I noticed an alarm clock for sale on the shelf behind him. He eventually got aggravated with me and loudly said, "Do you wanna screw for that"? I yelled back, "No! But I'd blow you for that alarm clock". He turned red as a beet and his co-worker father started screaming at him. After talking to a few co-workers, I found out that his Dad and I were probably the only ones who didn't know he was a butt pirate. Not that there's anything wrong with that. It took several days for me to work up the nerve to send a friend over for the screw.

LUNCH WITH THE PRESIDENT

╽┥╸╆╸╆╸╆╸╆╸╋╸╋╸╈┥

U NLIKE FLIGHT CREWS THAT ARE PUT UP IN HO-
tels on their layovers, train crews often find themselves sharing a bunk in train station crew rooms.
However, several years ago, our railroad was unable to
provide bunk space for our train crews. The railroad temporarily put us up in a nice hotel right across from our
terminal. The hotel had a policy that if they didn't have a
room immediately available for a crewmember they gave
you a voucher for lunch in their fancy, expensive restaurant. This allowed flight crews or in this case train crews
to kill some time while waiting for a room to become
available. The same one or two guys always seemed to
figure out a way to time their arrival so as to get a free

lunch. Despite the fact I had bonded with Rachel, the young lady at the front desk, I had never received a lunch voucher. One morning I showed up for a key to a room and Rachel winked at me, telling me there was only one room left. She said that if I took a walk around the block, it would probably be gone and I could get lunch on them. Sure enough, I had my first lunch voucher. We're talking fancy, schmancy stuff. I noticed that the hotel's restaurant had a pastrami sandwich on the menu that cost over $30.00. I knew I'd never spend that much of my own money on a sandwich so I figured I would check it out. Probably because they knew I was a freeloader, they sat me at a table that accommodated just one diner and that left me facing a wall. As I waited for my millionaire's sandwich I heard a commotion behind me. A few guys in dark suits entered first. They had earpieces and looked like Secret Service agents. A very short guy with a fancy suit and even fancier mustache followed them. Behind him were armed soldiers. Their entourage commandeered about of a third of the restaurant. For some reason they didn't ask me to change tables. Instead the little guy with the armed guards sat down right behind me so we were back to back. One of the big guys in the suits squished right between us with his back to me and his butt right up by the back of my head. I reached my head around him and said hello to the little guy who just smiled back. I watched them bring the little fella a shrimp cocktail with crustaceans the size of baseballs. When I saw him receive a second serving I reached around and said, "you sure must like shrimp". Once again, he smiled but didn't reply. The guard however, shot me a look like he was ready to kill me. Since I'm an idiot, I asked the guard if he could move over a little saying that if he blew a fart, he might knock me through the wall. He glared at me and needless to say, didn't move. The look in his eyes scared the crap out of me, so I figured I'd keep my mouth shut the rest of the time and just finish my sandwich. On my way out, I stopped to thank Rachel and I asked her who the big-shot midget was. She laughed and said that he's the owner of the hotel and by the way, also the President of Pakistan, Pervez Musharraf. Holy crap! I could have started an international incident with a nuclear-armed country.

The rest of my day was uneventful, until my last trip home. Nearing the last stop, I noticed a small group of guys heading down the aisle towards me. One, overly good looking fellow was stopping to shake hands with the passengers. Eventually a member of their entourage with a video camera made his way to me and asked me to pose with candidate Rick Lazio. I said, "Who the heck is Rick Lazio"? He replied that Rick Lazio was running for United States Senator. I told him I was busy working and didn't have time for a photo op. Furthermore, I watched his jaw drop when I told him that I had just had lunch with the President of Pakistan and didn't have time for a Senator!

P.S. Musharraf went on to make the news quite a bit. Rick Lazio lost to Hillary Clinton in his campaign for the U.S. Senate.... and the pastrami was delicious.

THE END OF THE LINE

┡┽┽┽┽┽┽┽┽┥

I WILL GREATLY MISS MANY OF MY REGULAR PASSEN-gers. There was Carl the Wonder Dog, an old retiree who always had a corny joke (if the Bronx Zoo sold all their wildebeests would that mean no gnus is good gnus?), Railroad Jack, who is a great guy who endeared himself to me despite being a rail nut, and Cheesecake Jimmy, a dapper fellow in his late 80's who would put on a fine suit and top hat and ride into the city just to pick up cheesecakes for the people he cared about, which always included his conductor. I had a special affection for one tall, old guy who would start screaming that he was a war veteran if you tried to collect his fare. I realized after a while that he was actually off his rocker when he came to believe that he was a Rabbi. Even though he wasn't Jewish, he would wear a yarmulke and act the part. Once I realized he was nuts I would just wish him a "good morning Rabbi" and he would respond back "good Yom Tov" (good holiday).

The passenger I'll miss most of all is known by the name of Rocky. Rocky's been riding our trains since he was a little kid. He's not so little anymore, standing about 6'7" in heels. Yup. Heels. He's scared more than a few commuters when darting out of the bathroom after a quick change into stilettos and fishnets. Rocky has become a beloved mascot of our conductors and was like the brother I never had.

Separated at birth? The resemblance is uncanny!

With his size and strength, young goons quickly learned not to pick on Rocky. He was renowned for coming to the defense of our train crews. On one late night train, two thug passengers were threatening a conductor. When the conductor stepped out onto the station platform, he wasn't aware that the guys had snuck up behind him and one had a knife drawn. Rocky saw what was happening and quickly high heeled it out onto the platform. He closed in behind the guy who was wielding the knife, put his giant hands on his shoulders and crushed him down to the ground. He slammed the second guy into the station's wall. The guys took one look at Rocky and couldn't figure out whether to whimper or run. Another conductor got into an argument with a rider that was about to escalate into a fistfight. Rocky got between them and said with his unique voice, "You leave my friend alone". The guy took one look at this 6'7" muscular guy, wearing fishnets and a Tina Turner wig and ran like the wind. While appearances might be deceiving, Rocky is a good man with a gentle soul. However, regardless of whether he or a train crew member was the intended victim, he never took kindly to bullies. In one well-known incident, he was being verbally abused and shoved around by five passengers who were obvious thugs. They made the unfortunate mistake of assuming his choice of attire inferred that he was an easy target for a bigoted beat-down. Fortunately the train was stopped at a station instead of on the move when Rocky threw two of them through an emergency window (without first opening it). Ultimately, three of the thugs were taken away on stretchers. Rocky found himself in handcuffs but was quickly released when the train crew and passengers explained that he was in fact the victim of the assault. Good man that Rocky. Rocky was there when I started on the railroad and he was still riding the rails when I packed it in. Maybe when I really pack it in, my friends and family can have a funeral pyre, with Dust in the Wind playing and Rocky dancing around the fire in full regalia.

Rocky ~ 6'7" of Rail Royalty!

EPILOGUE

I LEFT THE RAILROAD, NO LONGER A YOUNG BUCK but a rather a well-seasoned conductor. However, I can joyously report that life remains funny, even once you've blossomed into an old rear end.

Late in my career I was trying to stay awake on an early morning train by sucking on a peppermint lifesaver. After just a minute or two, these popular little candies tend to break up into three or four smaller pieces in your mouth. A passenger showed me his ticket and I replied "thanks". Unfortunately, as I said "thanks" a little piece of white lifesaver popped out of my mouth and landed on the seat right beside him. The rider almost had a nervous breakdown in what seemed to be a complete overreaction. It turned out he overreacted because he thought his old geezer conductor had spit out a tooth!

This book has been a microcosm of my career from start to finish. This was never more evident than when I sought out a pair of white boxer shorts with red hearts for a possible cover photo. I put the word out to my fellow conductors in an effort to borrow a pair. Having read this book, it probably won't surprise you to learn that a ridiculous number of my co-workers own a pair of Valentine's Day bloomers. What really summed it up was when a young lady conductor met a southbound train at a station in upstate New York. She handed the train's engineer a large envelope containing a pair of women's undies with red lips printed on them. She then informed him that I would be meeting the train in Grand Central to pick up her underwear. Railroader's are a unique and great bunch in that he didn't even bat an eye.

Some folks feel terrible when they get railroaded but for me it's been the ride of a lifetime. Thanks for coming along and remember to watch the gap!

ACKNOWLEDGEMENTS

I AM EXTREMELY APPRECIATIVE OF MY WIFE FOR ALlowing me to tell my story, and our progeny, Amy for her incomparable editing, Dan for his vernacular suggestions and Nicole for losing a screw, thereby providing a chapter. Thank you to my friends and co-workers, including Tammy Smith, Doug Mullen, Mike Shaw, Anthony Aprea, Mike Cunningham, Mike Cifu, and Bob Lafreniere for their input. Much deserved cover photo credit to Jim Kincade and Del Lorenzo, Jason Gleis (GCT photo) and Ken Houghton Rail Images. I would like to express my gratitude to Richard Aquan, Susan Turner, and author Nicholas Borelli for their incredible talent and guidance. Last but certainly not least, thank you to Rocky, the best commuter in the world, for his sense of humor and loyalty to our train crews.

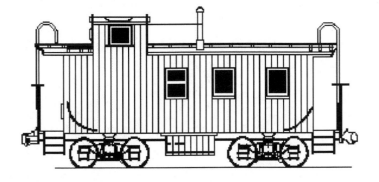